Thomas Jefferson
ARCHITECT

Other books by Hugh Howard

Wright for Wright (with Roger Straus III)
House-Dreams
The Preservationist's Progress
How Old Is This House?
Bob Vila's Complete Guide to Remodeling Your House

Other books by Roger Straus III

Wright for Wright (with Hugh Howard)
Modernism Reborn (with Michael Webb)
U.S. 1: America's Original Main Street (with Andrew H. Malcolm)
Mississippi Currents (with Andrew H. Malcolm)

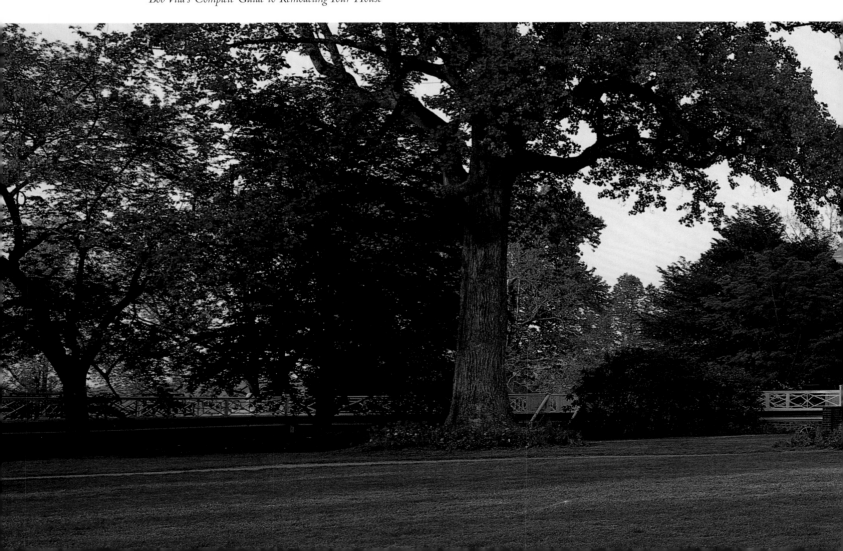

Thomas Jefferson
ARCHITECT
THE BUILT LEGACY OF OUR THIRD PRESIDENT

Text by HUGH HOWARD *Photographs by* ROGER STRAUS III

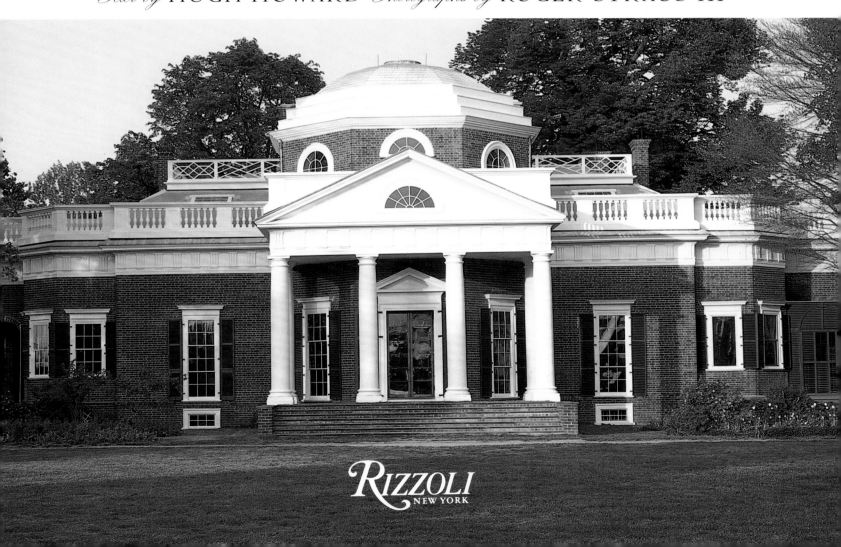

RIZZOLI
NEW YORK

First published in the United States of America in 2003 by
RIZZOLI INTERNATIONAL PUBLICATIONS, INC.
300 Park Avenue South, New York, NY 10010
This edition published in 2015.

ISBN: 978-0-8478-4539-2
LCCN: 2014950348

Cover photograph: The Rotunda at the University of Virgina, Charlottesville (p. 132)
Endpapers: Rendering of the west elevation of Monticello, Charlottesville (p. 56)
Title page photograph: The garden façade at Monticello, Charlottesville (p. 26)

Designed by Doris Straus

Printed and bound in China

2015 2016 2017 2018 / 10 9 8 7 6 5 4 3 2 1

Contents

"A temple in the woods," said Sir Kenneth Clarke of Fiske Kimball's home, Shack Mountain.

For my father, Roger W. Straus

— R. S.

and in memory of Mimi, Martha Vincent Miller Lawrence

— H. H.

Preface

$\mathcal{F}$inding the perfect title for this book was a simple matter, but deciding to use it was more difficult. From the start, *Thomas Jefferson, Architect* was the favored title because it identifies precisely what this book presumes to be. Yet *Thomas Jefferson, Architect* comes with an unwanted sense of presumption.

The difficulty was posed by another book with the same name. Published in 1916, Fiske Kimball's *Thomas Jefferson, Architect*, made available Jefferson's previously unknown architectural drawings. The combination of the plates and Kimball's pioneering research introduced the world to the notion that Mr. Jefferson was an architect – as strange as it may seem today, his architectural influence was largely unacknowledged a century ago. Kimball's book quickly became a cornerstone of Jefferson studies, and Kimball established himself as a scholar, curator, restoration advisor, and architect in his own right. He will reprise some of those roles in this book, too, but let's return to his book for a moment.

Produced by The Riverside Press in Cambridge, Massachusetts, *Thomas Jefferson, Architect* is long out print. First edition copies of the elephant folio are dear indeed today, as the rare copy that surfaces of the original press run (a mere 350 copies) invariably commands thousands of dollars. Copies from a reprint edition published by The Da Capo Press in 1968 also appear only through rare book dealers, typically at prices in the mid-three figures. It was, in part, the very rarity of Kimball's book that emboldened us to adopt his title, but there was another factor, too.

In writing this book, the need to distinguish Jefferson's labors as a designer-builder from his other accomplishments became apparent. Early on I found the epithet "Thomas Jefferson, Architect" appearing involuntarily in my drafts. At first the construction seemed awkward, but over a period of months I grew accustomed to its usefulness in reminding the reader of the focus of this book. Perhaps inevitably, then, this book became *Thomas Jefferson, Architect,* and that makes a couple of disclaimers necessary.

We do not claim to offer in this volume the kind of ground-breaking scholarship Kimball did (although Jefferson studies is a field so vigorously worked by scholars that new understandings regularly come to light, and every attempt has been made in writing this book to reflect the best current understandings of Jefferson and Jeffersonian buildings). This volume will not supercede Kimball's landmark volume, though its color photographs, taken specifically for its publication, can only enhance appreciation of Jefferson's buildings as they are today, rather than in Jefferson's time (or, for that matter, in Kimball's). Our hope is this book will find its own place in the Jefferson literature, being of utility to scholars for its broad overview and, more importantly, that this *Thomas Jefferson, Architect* will nurture in a larger public the growing fascination with Mr. Jefferson and his buildings that Sidney Fiske Kimball initiated.

–H. H.

A Note on the Photographs

I used three cameras for making the photographs in this book. My principle camera was a Plaubel 69W proshift fitted with a Schneider Super-Angulon 5.6/47 lens. The panoramas were done with a Linhof Technorama 617 S with a Schneider Super-Angulon 5.6/90 lens. For handheld shots, I used a Leica R7. I worked with two lens on the Leica, a Vario-Elmar 3.5/35-70 and a APO-Telyt-R 3.4/180. My film was Fujichrome 100F and 400F for low light conditions. I think Mr. Jefferson would have been amused by all these gadgets.

–R. S.

Introduction

*I*n Jefferson's aspirations lie his greatness. He imagined a legal framework whereby the colonies would separate from England. The written document that resulted was the Declaration of Independence.

He helped shape the republic in its early years as Washington's secretary of state and John Adams' vice president. Upon becoming President himself, his vision for his country led him to make the Louisiana Purchase, doubling the land area of the United States. He went on to create the University of Virginia.

Throughout his life he sought better solutions, higher knowledge, and

Tuckahoe, Jefferson's only surviving childhood home.

even truth and beauty as an accomplished horticulturalist, inventor, scientist, ambassador, bibliographer, and connoisseur of food, wine, and the arts. He played the violin, studied the stars, set broken limbs, and performed vaccinations. More than any American he personified the Enlightenment. At a time when it was almost possible for one man to know about everything, Thomas Jefferson came surprisingly close.

The purpose of this book, however, is to examine a single element of a much larger life. Our thesis here is quite simple, that Thomas Jefferson was an architect of great skill and immense influence. Not that the buildings of Thomas Jefferson, Architect, can be separated from the rest of his life and work. In fact, as one of the great political thinkers of all time, Jefferson allowed his political conscience to influence his architecture. In self-conscious fashion he sought by architectural means to inculcate the citizens of his new country with classical ideals.

To put it rather crudely, he came along and said, 'Hey, let's get classical!' And a great many Americans have been following his lead ever since. Thanks largely to Jefferson, classical architecture became America's de facto governmental mode of building. The first public monument in the classical style in the United States was the Virginia Capitol, and Jefferson was its designer. He modeled it after a temple built by the ancient Romans. As secretary of state when Washington, D.C., was in the planning stages, he influenced the design not only of the city but of many major monuments, including the White House and the Capitol. Today the Supreme Court, most statehouses, and thousands of schools, courthouses, and municipal buildings are classical, too. Step off the time machine any time in the last two hundred years and you will find American dwellings that have been built in the same spirit, ranging from Gone-with-the-Wind mansions in the south to mill workers' housing and farmhouses in the north, and, reaching into in the twentieth century, millions of suburban homes often described as "colonial." We can't give Jefferson all the credit, of course, but America never had a more effective cheerleader for things classical.

Architecture as Jefferson saw it was more than a matter of buildings. The style he developed, now commonly referred to as "Jeffersonian Classicism," embraced both Roman architectural notions and republican ideals. It was a reaction against things British, specifically the Georgian style which, not accidentally, got its name from the hated English kings. Jefferson and others found the analogy between the newly independent nation and the Roman republic congenial. There was an easy logic to adopting the form of classical temples not only for civic buildings but for dwellings, too, thereby affirming a connection to Greek democracy and Roman political institutions (ironically, though, many of the Roman monuments dated from the time of the Roman Empire rather than the Republic).

What Americans have always admired about Thomas Jefferson is his independence of mind. Yet his belief in personal and religious freedom, in free enterprise and economic opportunity was not based upon a desire to reinvent the world. On the contrary, Jefferson wanted to revert to a storybook time characterized by personal freedom and social harmony, a simpler time when men lived off the land in peace. He believed that the English monarchy stood between the colonists and an opportunity to recapture a paradisaical past where reason ruled. The first step in understanding Jefferson is to apprehend that he cherished the lessons of the past.

His biography is chockablock with examples. To cite just one, his independent thinking led him to devise his own system of classification for his library. He divided knowledge into three principal "faculties," they being

Memory (subtitled History), Reason (Philosophy), and Imagination (Fine Arts). There are further subdivisions, but the three main headings neatly characterize Jefferson's world view, as well as his attitude toward most everything, including architecture. For him, shaping a country or a building involved looking first to the past; reason and imagination came after. As we will see, Jefferson's buildings are nothing if not thoughtful and artistic – but always within a historic context.

In broad strokes, Jefferson's biography runs this way. He was born in Charlottesville in April of 1743, the first son of Peter Jefferson and Jane Randolph. After a childhood spent at his father's plantation, Shadwell, and at Tuckahoe, an estate in the Randolph family, he attended the College of William and Mary for two years, graduating in 1762. He remained in Williamsburg to read law and was admitted to the bar in 1767. He returned to Charlottesville to practice law and married Martha Wayles Skelton in 1771. She bore him five children, two of whom would survive to adulthood. Before the Revolution he was elected to the Virginia Assembly and during the conflict became Governor of Virginia. His wife died in 1782, and he never remarried. In 1784 he departed for Europe, and served as Minister to France until 1789. On returning home, he accepted Washington's appointment as secretary of state, a job he performed until 1793. He was elected vice president in 1797 and thereafter was elected to the presidency for two terms (1801–1809). He retired to tend his plantations, but from 1817 until his death 1826 he was deeply engaged in establishing the University of Virginia.

These bare facts convey little of how or why Jefferson became an architectural avatar. Very likely a key episode was a building campaign at his Shadwell home when he was ten, a perfect age for a boy to be enraptured by the sight of a wooden frame rising atop a stone foundation to become a dwelling. We know few details of what he saw because in 1770 a great fire consumed the house. The fire influenced Jefferson, too, as he would later dismiss wood construction as ugly and perishable in his book, *Notes on the State of Virginia*. No doubt he did so in part because of his experience with losing not only the house but the entire written record of his early years. The painful lesson certainly contributed to his selection of brick as the material of choice for the buildings he designed.

Another influence on Jefferson was his education, which included an early introduction to Latin as a schoolboy. At age fourteen, his father died and the younger Jefferson's studies shifted to a log schoolhouse near Shadwell where, Jefferson later recalled, he got a thorough grounding in Greek as well as Latin. His classical education introduced him to Latin authors imbued with the monuments of Rome, and as an adult he read both ancient languages with skill and satisfaction. Historians have observed that the Founding Fathers probably knew more of classical antiquity than they did of contemporary Europe or even other parts of their own land. Jefferson was no exception.

Although he died when Thomas was an adolescent, Peter Jefferson's influence is to be read in his son's life. The older man had been a surveyor who, together with a mathematics teacher at William and Mary, Joshua Fry, prepared a map of Virginia in 1751. Jefferson was justifiably proud of his father's work, as the map remained the standard for decades and Jefferson himself reprinted it in *Notes on the State of Virginia* in 1787. Upon his father's death, Jefferson inherited some 5,000 acres from his father but his inheritance seems also to have come with a dose of the discipline that had made the father a first-rate surveyor. The desire to put an accurate topo-

≪ TUCKAHOE ≫

As adults, we can reach only so far into our memories. But if Jefferson were alive to think back on his youth, no doubt his recollections would first come into focus at Tuckahoe. That plantation, located in Goochland County near Richmond, was home for much of his childhood, probably from 1746 through 1757, the year of his father's death. Tuckahoe is believed to have been built in two phases, probably in 1723 and 1734.

Tuckahoe was one of several Randolph plantations, and Jefferson arrived there when his father moved his own family to fulfill a promise to raise Thomas's cousin, the orphan Thomas Mann Randolph. Randolph would become a life long friend and, many years later, an in-law as well as a cousin when Jefferson's older daughter, Martha, married Thomas Mann Randolph, Jr. Tuckahoe was also a stop on Jefferson's own wedding trip in 1772, so the house was an on-again, off-again presence in Jefferson's life.

In his writings, Jefferson was quick to dismiss wood-frame Virginia homes as impermanent and lacking in style and, by default, Tuckahoe was lumped in with the rest. Yet in the way that childhood homes invariably do, Tuckahoe exercised a significant — if rather subliminal — influence on Jefferson's thinking. The resemblance in particular between Tuckahoe and the layout of Monticello II (see page 47) has been the subject of some intriguing scholarly conjecture. Like the fully evolved Monticello, Tuckahoe had a scheme in which its saloon, the primary public room on the ground floor, served as a buffer through which only certain privileged visitors would pass. The visitors who made the first cut were invited to the public wing, while the private family quarters remained separate, a third zone in the house. When Jefferson remade Monticello in the 1790s, its new program echoed Tuckahoe's: it had a filtering hall, a sequence of rooms for entertaining, and his distinctly private quarters. Tuckahoe was the first gracious house in his experience and seems to have had a greater influence on his architectural thinking than even he realized.

Jefferson certainly didn't copy the grand stairway at Tuckahoe — the stairs at Monticello were "suppressed," tall and narrow affairs shoe-horned into passageways — but he would have admired its superb workmanship.

Only seven years after the initial construction phase, a second wing (right) and a connecting hyphen were added to Tuckahoe. The hyphen contained the saloon for greeting visitors and, on special occasions, a gracious space for entertaining. Very likely one wing became a public space for certain guests, the other family quarters.

graphical record on paper of natural and man-made features reemerged in the son. The younger man was driven to design buildings, a discipline that also involved the creation of two-dimensional paperwork renderings of three-dimensional places.

When Jefferson went to college at sixteen, the journey was a revelation. He had never visited a town of any size, and Williamsburg was then the capital of Virginia, home to the royal governor, and a bustling market town. If at first Williamsburg seemed a great metropolis to Jefferson, however, it wasn't. The population in 1758 was about a thousand, roughly half slaves, with members of the gentry numbering only in the dozens (in comparison London's population was then approaching three-quarters of a million people). But as the capital of England's richest American colony, it boasted a stylish Governor's Palace and a Capitol, as well as Jefferson's destination, the College of William of Mary. His years in Williamsburg also exposed him to well-traveled mentors, including the royal governor, Francis Fauquier, and to the homes of such friends as John Page whose family seat, Rosewell, was among the finest colonial houses of the era.

These retrospective observations – that Jefferson witnessed the Shadwell build, that he developed a passion for Roman writers, that he had a draftsman dad, and the revelation of Williamsburg's streetscapes on his arrival there – offer no moment of epiphany in the birth of Jefferson's architectural consciousness. They are little more than after-the-fact interpretations of circumstances, and Jefferson himself, rarely an introspective man, never characterized for posterity the moment he conceived his passion for buildings. Yet one event was recorded by his tutor, sometime secretary, and enduring friend William Short. It occurred in Williamsburg during Jefferson's first year at college.

Short remembered a visit of Jefferson's to a cabinetmaker who lived near the college gate. Already a rabid collector, the adolescent Jefferson made the call seeking an old book. The tradesman, having become more interested in booze than books, was persuaded to part with the tome Jefferson wanted. The old folio Jefferson carried back to his rooms was the first of many architecture volumes Jefferson would acquire. We can only conjecture as to what book it was, since Jefferson's first library (he assembled three in his lifetime) was lost in the Shadwell fire on February 1, 1770. Scholars have hypothesized that it may have been Robert Morris's *Select Architecture* or James Gibbs' *Rules for Drawing the Several Parts of Architecture*, a pair of eighteenth-century English books Jefferson would own and that are thought to have been sources for his principal home, Monticello, which he soon began to design. Still other students of Jefferson have concluded that the book he purchased that day was an English translation of Andrea Palladio's *I Quattro Libri dell'Architettura*, which had originally been published in Venice in 1570.

The Four Books on Architecture fits the larger narrative of Jefferson's life perfectly. He himself later called it his "Bible" for architectural matters, and the influence of its plates and text can be read in virtually all of his designs. Palladio truly became a spiritual guide for Thomas Jefferson, Architect, an *éminence grise* whose book was always near to guide Jefferson's hand. Jefferson's encounter with *The Four Books* – whether it transpired on the day Short recalled or on some other – just may have been the moment of discovery when Jefferson felt emboldened to become an architect.

No visitor can venture far into Jefferson territory without encountering his oft-quoted words, "Putting up and pulling down [is] one of my favorite amusements." The phrase feels particularly apropos at Monticello, and the

✎ THE WREN BUILDING ✎

The Wren building got its name from the distinguished seventeenth-century English architect, Christopher Wren, once thought to have been its designer. Built between 1695 and 1700 to house the College of William and Mary, the building today appears much as it did when Jefferson was a student there. As with several of the high-style buildings he knew in his youth, including Rosewell and the Governor's Palace (see opposite and page 16), this building failed to excite Jefferson's tastes — he said of the Wren building that it was but a "rude, mis-shapen pile."

During Jefferson's years of reading law in Williamsburg, his erudition and maturity won him a frequent place at the table of the royal governor, Francis Fauquier. Fauquier was a fellow of the Royal Society and, as well as being a man possessed of scientific curiosity, he had a cultured taste for music and conversation. Jefferson later acknowledged the lessons learned in Fauquier's company: The Governor's Palace was, Jefferson wrote, "the finest school of manners and morals that ever existed in America."

While he was always reserved in assessing the early architecture of Williamsburg, Jefferson may have had Fauquier to thank for helping to kindle his nascent interest in buildings. The royal governor's previous landlord in London had been none other than James Gibbs, the man who put a steeple on his London church, St. Martin-in-the-Fields, and in doing so inspired the countless early churches in the United States (the combination of the classical portico topped by a Baroque steeple was Gibb's innovation).

Years later, when the Palace became his residence as the elected governor of Virginia, Jefferson the tireless remodeler could not resist redesigning the Palace in a less baroque vein. The urge to renovate came over him in virtually all of his residences (not only at Monticello, but even in his temporary quarters in Philadelphia, New York, in Paris at the Hôtel de Langeac, and later at the building we know today as the White House). Ironically, the five drawings he left behind for the unexecuted remodeling of the Governor's Palace into a neoclassical building proved of inestimable value in the twentieth century when the structure, which had burned in 1781, was recreated by Colonial Williamsburg.

product people at the Thomas Jefferson Memorial Foundation sensed this, too. On my first visit to Monticello some years ago, a T-shirt bearing just those words was on sale at the gift shop.

Anyone who knows the history of Monticello understands Jefferson spoke the words literally. Yet there's a subtext, too, within Jefferson's memorable turn of phrase. The key is the word "amusements." Its usage hasn't changed since Jefferson's time; then, as now, an amusement was an entertainment, a diversion. Jefferson regarded architecture as a bit like chess, his favorite game, to which there is also a geometrical joy. Perhaps music belongs in the mix as another of Jefferson's passions and one that, again, like architecture, operates at a mathematical level. While he took each of them seriously, he pursued architecture, chess, and music because they were pleasurable escapes for him. Thus, despite the influence that his designs have had, architecture must be seen as a Jefferson avocation, a favored hobby of a man of capacious intellect.

That put him very much in step with his time. In eighteenth-century America, there were no professional

Rosewell may have been the grandest colonial house of its time. Jefferson knew it well, having visited the estate often in the company of John Page, his close friend and William and Mary classmate. Rosewell was a convenient escape for the two students, a short ferry ride across the York River from Williamsburg.

Constructed in 1726, the thirty-room house must have been a remarkable sight. The walls of the three-story structure were immensely tall, and Rosewell's impressive profile was made more so by the twin octagonal lanterns set atop its flat roof like matching crowns. One was a summer house where Jefferson spent much time with his friend, taking in the spectac-

ular gardens below and the broad river views beyond. Cut Portland stone imported from England was used to finish the window lintels, chimneys, and doorways at Rosewell. The brickwork was of the highest standard, too, featuring rubbed, gauged, and molded bricks. In fact, when Jefferson set about making bricks for Monticello, he referred back to the masonry he had seen at Rosewell.

Inside the house stood an imposing and exquisitely carved staircase of a quality rarely found in America at the time. Few callers ever got to climb that staircase, as the hall also functioned as a screening area for visitors in this aristocratic home. While Rosewell, like Jefferson's Monticello, was an aspirational house, the Pages chose to echo high-style English practices of the time. In contrast, Jefferson's later designs had a more democratic message to convey. Rosewell, then, fits into Jefferson's architectural mindscape because of the many ways in which he elected not to imitate it. The Pages wanted Rosewell to remind the visitor of their wealth and power, so they hired English masons and carpenters to execute what was literally a London town-house design, down to stone and brick elements dictated by contemporary London fire-prevention regulations.

Much altered over the centuries, Rosewell burned in 1916. What remains resembles great brick pylons, towering over grassy mounds of fallen debris like some sort of bizarre burial monument. What survive, as well, are Jefferson's recollections of the place in his correspondence. In 1770, the very year that Jefferson moved to the south pavilion at Monticello, he wrote to John Page, himself a future governor of Virginia. Jefferson reminded his friend of the "philosophical evenings" they had spent at Rosewell watching the stars. While Jefferson was laboring over the designs for his mountain–top aerie, as he himself called it, he found himself recollecting their shared passion for astronomy. It is no accident that he elected not to copy English models but instead opted for a more visionary approach, which involved teaching his visitors not about wealth but of the classical past and the American future.

architects. The first architecture school didn't come into existence on American shores until the Institute of Technology (now MIT) established an architectural curriculum in 1865. A number of formally trained designers had arrived from Europe earlier, among them the Englishman Benjamin Latrobe (with whom Jefferson collaborated on several occasions) and the Irishman James Hoban, the architect of the White House. But in the early years of the republic self-taught amateurs like William Thornton, the first designer of the Capitol in Washington and a doctor by profession, and owner-builders such as Jefferson and George Washington set the architectural tone in the new nation.

Although Jefferson must be regarded as an amateur, that is not to disparage him as a dabbler. His life-long devotion to design and buildings refutes that suggestion. He was an amateur in the eighteenth-century sense meaning one who loves or is fond of something. The word evolved from the French and Latin (in Latin, *amator* means a lover or devotee, and certainly Jefferson had a great affection for architecture). He was also an amateur in the more modern sense that he took no pay for his design work. That would have been to defy the rules of his gentlemanly status.

In Jefferson's day, as now, there was a division in architecture between the imagining of the building and its actual construction. First came the pen-and-pencils stage at which the design was conceived and put on paper. Subsequently the bricks-and-mortar, hammer-and-nail building process transformed two-dimensional paperwork into a three-dimensional structure. Ordinary houses – scholars term them "vernacular" architecture – are usually built more simply, since the builders are likely to have constructed similar houses before. But in high-style architecture the tradition has long been that the gentleman architect prepares the plans and the tradesman builder executes them. As Benjamin Latrobe wrote in 1806, American architecture then was "in the hands of two sorts of men . . . [those] who from traveling or from books have acquired some knowledge of the theory of the arts, – but who know nothing of its practice . . . [and those] whose early life being spent in labor . . . have had no opportunity of acquiring the theory."

Most members of Jefferson's class regarded building as better left to a lesser caste of tradesmen, but Jefferson was an exceptional case. He took great pains to design his house, producing more detailed plans than was typical of the time. He was endlessly interested in process, too, and followed the progress of building attentively. He asked questions, and sought to learn and understand how and why jobs were done in a certain way or a particular order. He made copious notes in his *Memorandum Books*, the household records he maintained for almost six decades. He had a work bench of his own in the piazza adjacent to his private quarters at Monticello. He worked with metal, shaping keys and chains in both iron and brass, and one French visitor reported that he frequently was "one of the builders." He also contributed to the joinery work on his carriage and some of his furniture.

In today's jargon, he could probably be termed a control freak. He was a time-and-motion specialist more than a century before the study of worker productivity became a standard industrial practice. He paid such close attention to details that few of his workers would have dared to carry out substantial tasks in his absence (this was one of a number of factors in the protracted building program at Monticello). He was a voluminous correspondent and his architecture-related papers have proven invaluable. Building records from the time are comparatively rare, since tradesmen were not always lettered, training was oral, and the work of building generally regarded as quotidian

❧ SHIRLEY PLANTATION ❧

Jefferson knew Shirley Plantation, having been a student at William and Mary with its owner, Charles Carter. Carter had remodeled the 1738 manor house, probably just before Jefferson's wedding, and Thomas and Martha Jefferson stayed here on their wedding trip in 1772. In the past some scholars hypothesized that Jefferson had a hand in its remodeling. Even though that seems unlikely, Shirley's double portico certainly resembles in broad outlines the frontispiece of the home Jefferson was planning and certainly he would have been struck by the quality of the workmanship at Shirley.

and unimportant. Thus Jefferson's records are a boon not only to the restorers of his buildings but to students of the building arts. He often took great pains to prescribe exactly what he wanted, specifying species of wood, thickness, and even nailing patterns. Jefferson, in short, was constitutionally adapted to be a builder as well as a designer.

His hands-on knowledge helped make his buildings possible. He was, after all, attempting to introduce designs from ancient Rome and Renaissance Italy to Albemarle County, a region where, as he would proudly recall, his own father had been one of the first settlers. Most of his builders came to him with little or no knowledge of classical columns, capitals, and cornices; these were men who had built vernacular houses of local materials that he dismissed as "ugly, uncomfortable, and . . . perishable." A man without Jefferson's thorough knowledge of how the parts were assembled would never have accomplished what he did. A fast learner, he quickly found himself becoming an unofficial teacher. His tutelage at Monticello, Poplar Forest, and the University of Virginia produced an impressive cadre of "undertakers," men skilled in the sophisticated, stylish architecture he prescribed (builders were then known as "undertakers" because they *undertook* a job). When these men fanned out from Charlottesville in the years after his death, they assured the survival of his architectural legacy through the construction of countless other buildings.

Jefferson reveled in being a child of the Enlightenment. He delighted in the notion that there were natural laws and a universal order which human reason could comprehend and employ in resolving social, political, and economic issues. After all, the Declaration of Independence, the consensus choice as his most significant accomplishment, is a bracing exercise in pure reason ("We hold these Truths to be self-evident . . ."). Jefferson wrote it, aptly enough, in the time known as the Age of Reason.

In a less self-confident era, one might see a certain hubris in his utter rationalism. He went about his life confidently measuring and calculating, recording in minute detail the data of his life and of those around him. In his *Memorandum Books* he noted in painstaking detail monies expended, the produce from his garden, exact counts of bricks laid per day, and precise observations of the productivity of his slaves and other workers. These journals are an invaluable reference for scholars reconstructing the events of a life. But there's a larger sense there, as well, of Jefferson's confidence in man's progress and perfectability.

He truly believed it was possible to live in harmony with the universe. In his view, the world in general could be made better and, in particular, he was persuaded there was ample room for improvement in the state of Virginia architecture. When considering the buildings of Williamsburg he dismissed the Palace as "not handsome," and said of the college buildings and Williamsburg's hospital "but that they have roofs, [they] would be taken for brick-kilns." He was convinced he could help rectify this sad state of affairs.

Jefferson scholars today shy away from claims that he was a great inventor. The code word they use instead is "tinkerer." Various machines that were once said to be of his imagining – he made no such claims but subsequent idolaters did – have generally proven to be the work of others. In some instances, however, Jefferson did make useful suggestions that improved existing devices such as the polygraph, the machine that simultaneously produced an original and a duplicate of a letter. In the same way, he made bold statements in his architectural work, mixing and matching in imaginative ways while drawing unabashedly on the work of others (and crediting his sources willingly). That separates him from many architects of the twentieth century for whom originality was everything. Frank Lloyd Wright made a positive fetish out of disclaiming any debt to the designers of the past; the builders of glass houses did what couldn't be done before; Frank Gehry and others have taken space-age materials and shaped them into never-before-seen forms. For better or for worse, the twentieth century had more than a few "because-I-can" buildings, structures built, at least in part, as an expression of new, unprecedented possibilities.

Jefferson, in contrast, began with the assumption that the lessons of the past were essential to good design. He wanted very much to believe, in the great tradition of Newton's laws of gravity and motion, that simple formulas could be learnt that guaranteed a right and satisfying design. Buildings, in short, should be built according to established rules. This wasn't some sort of early building code devised to assure safety; these rules were aesthetic. Along with his adopted mentor Palladio he was concerned with proportion, symmetry, and balance. Jefferson adopted from his architectural books the Renaissance orientation, the belief that the ancients had attained perfection by imitating "Nature" in their buildings. He promoted the notion that builders in his era could do the same if they could but follow the commandments, and he practiced what he preached. He found in Palladio's *Four Books* – and, specifically, in the first book – the guidance he needed.

Recall that Jefferson had been trained as a lawyer; the law is nothing if not a formal codification of customs that helps order society. He became a revolutionary in part because he regarded actions of King George III as unlawful (for example, taxation without representation). Even when in revolutionary mode he was considered and deliberate. Architecture, too, is about precedents and laws – and Thomas Jefferson, Architect, knew intuitively that nowhere in his life had he a better chance at achieving order than in architecture.

To understand Thomas Jefferson, Architect, one must know something of Andrea Palladio (1508-1580) and his work. If George Wythe was, as Jefferson recalled in his *Autobiography*, his "faithful and beloved mentor" in law and politics, then the sixteenth-century Italian was his favored tutor in matters architectural. Palladio had written that architecture should be ennobling; Jefferson, too, came to believe if you gave people good examples, if you put them in the right environments, that they would be improved by the experience. Jefferson's architectural eye admired the buildings limned in Palladio's drawings, but his political imagination was fired by Palladio's rhetoric about civilization and the nobility of agriculture.

Palladio's brief bio runs this way. He was born Andrea Della Gondola in the Veneto, the region that surrounds the low-lying mud archipelago that is Venice. His expectations were limited although he wasn't born to poverty (his father was a miller whose name reflected his ownership of a boat in which he made deliveries). At thirteen the son was apprenticed to learn the trade of stone cutting, but in his early twenties Andrea's talents caught the eye of Gion Giorgio Trissino. Count Trissino rebaptized the young stone mason with the new surname Palladio, guided his study of humanist philosophy, and inspired in him a taste for classical ideals and forms. He also took him to Rome to see the monuments of antiquity, hired him to remodel his own villa, and then arranged for other, important architectural commissions.

Thanks to Trissino, Palladio embarked upon a long career. His emergence as a brilliant designer coincided with a need for villas on the Veneto, where wealthy Venetian families had large land holdings. The key to under-

A signer of the Declaration of Independence, George Wythe (1726-1806) resided in this impressive and stylish Georgian house throughout Jefferson's Williamsburg years. The younger man knew its proportions, finish, and even furnishings (very likely a dining table and seven chairs at Monticello came from Wythe). In his will, Wythe bequeathed Jefferson his "books and small philosophical apparatus," a gesture symbolic of a larger intellectual gift the wise and worldly Wythe had already given. Jefferson himself described Wythe as "my faithful and beloved Mentor in youth, and my most affectionate friend through life," yet he chose not to imitate the grand but stolid character of Wythe's Williamsburg home.

standing Palladio's genius is the recognition that he adapted the ideas of ancient Rome to building farmhouses, albeit palatial ones. Palladio was actually an early archaeologist who, on his five trips to Rome, visited great Roman temples, many of them ruins, and measured their columns, pilasters, pediments, and domes. When he returned home, he designed *All'antica*, that is, "in the antique manner." He became the first great architect to devote much of his practice to designing houses, and he adapted classical forms, including the temple front and the dome, to domestic architecture. Eventually he put on paper the lessons he had inferred from his investigations, which included rules that specified, for example, that columns of a certain height had to be a certain diameter.

Palladio himself drew upon earlier writers, including the Roman Vitruvius whose *de Architectura* is the only surviving treatise on architecture from antiquity. Palladio illustrated an important edition of that work in 1567, then followed with his own *Four Books of Architecture* in 1570. Both texts expound upon what makes buildings classical, the elements that Christopher Wren aptly described as the "Latin" of classical architecture. This classical grammar is derived from decorative features used in ancient Rome and Greece. The essential scheme of architectural classicism is embodied by "the orders," which are the various combinations of vertical posts and horizontal beams that constitute the structure of a classical building. Each order is easily distinguished by examining its posts or, more correctly, its columns. Palladio devoted the first of his *Four Books* to the five orders, they being Tuscan, Doric, Ionic, Corinthian, and Composite. The Ionic order is identifiable by the scroll-shaped volutes on its capital; acanthus leaves decorate Corinthian capitals; and the Composite features both volutes and leaves. The simpler Tuscan and Doric are differentiated by moldings. Each of the five orders has not only its own form of column but also distinctive decorations on the entablature, which may include triglyphs, dentils, and other decorations applied in horizontal bands just beneath the roof line.

The orders had evolved over the centuries. The Corinthian is thought to be an Athenian invention dating from the fifth century B.C.E., the Ionic from Asia Minor a century earlier. Each order brings with it distinct proportions, with the hearty Tuscan at one extreme and the more graceful, attenuated Composite at the other. For a designer – in antiquity, in the Renaissance, and for Jefferson – the choice of order expressed both the intention of the architect and the character of the building. The Tuscan conveyed a feeling of sturdiness, and was perfectly suited to practical buildings, simple homes or even barns. Moving up to the Doric, Ionic, Corinthian, or Composite conveyed increased power, prestige, and importance. In a sense, then, the classical architect had to learn to play by the orders.

Jefferson immediately felt at home with Palladio's prescriptions, which specified proportions, with column diameters determining column height, intercolumniation, and how tall the entablature was to stand. It didn't take all the mystery or fun out of the process, as Jefferson recognized in the first of Palladio's *Four Books* a grammar he could use to express himself. The architectural "laws" that Palladio calibrated and promulgated were not hard-and-fast, since by no means all of the buildings of antiquity conform to one simple set of rules. The orders as described by Palladio and other Renaissance writers like Sebastiano Serlio are surprisingly variable, and while some designers carefully copied ancient models in whole or in part, others used a thorough understanding of the orders as a starting point from which to venture, varying the details to suit their own purposes while respecting the spirit of the rules. Palladio, Serlio, Jefferson, and countless others believed that by honoring the orders of the "Antients" (Jefferson's spelling) that beautiful and satisfying buildings would result. The buildings speak for themselves.

Jefferson's circumstances as a plantation owner with an admiration of the classical past made him the perfect audience for Palladio's writings, and he became the chief proponent of Palladianism in America. Even a cursory comparison of Jefferson's designs and Palladio's *oeuvre* offers obvious parallels. Jefferson's first design for Monticello resembles Palladio's Villa Cornaro; the Capitol in Richmond is linked to the Maison Carrée, a Roman building Palladio recorded in *The Four Books*; the Pantheon in Rome to which Palladio devoted a chapter was later the basis for the Rotunda at Jefferson's University; and the Villa Rotunda, probably the best known of Palladio's villas, was an important inspiration for such disparate buildings as Monticello, Jefferson's proposed design for the President's House, and his second home, Poplar Forest.

If Palladio was the high priest and the orders his canon, then there were other holy men at hand, too, including the Englishman Robert Morris early in Jefferson's life and, later, the sixteenth-century French architect

The Orders, according to Palladio's contemporary, Sebastiano Serlio: The Tuscan, Doric, Ionic, Corinthian, and Composite.

Roland Fréart de Chambray. Jefferson worshiped the Roman architectural past as these and other writers recorded it (Jefferson himself never visited Rome), and he came to regard their books as sacred texts, essential tools for shaping his architectural vision. Yet to regard Jefferson as merely an apostle would be wrong.

His architectural career is full of firsts. His Capitol was the first public building in America with a temple front (meaning its face consisted of a row of columns supporting a triangular pediment above). The completed Monticello was topped by the first dome on a private residence in the United States, and Poplar Forest seems to have been the first octagonal house in America, too. Admittedly, he borrowed elements, sometimes copied, and often adapted them. But Jefferson reimagined them in an American and, more specifically, Virginian context. He rethought the scale of Palladian and Classical buildings. He was forced to adapt native brick and timber rather than use the stone or stucco of his models. In a provincial place where architecture was usually about ordinary people seeking shelter and builders constructing houses using their craft but little theory, Jefferson introduced an overarching intellectual construct. Paradoxically, though Jefferson's buildings were faithful to classical Palladianism, they emerged as distinctly American and notably Jeffersonian.

≪ THE WILLIAM FINNIE HOUSE ≫

The William Finnie house was built before 1782 and has long been recognized as among the most stylish houses in Williamsburg. Its tripartite design, with a central block and flanking wings, is trickle-down Palladian, probably adapted by local builders from English pattern books of the time. The Finnie House was thought to have been an early work of Jefferson, though today that attribution has been largely dismissed. Colonial Williamsburg Foundation.

A major challenge in considering Thomas Jefferson, Architect, is to balance the *known* and the *unknown*. Happily, his four principle architectural works survive, they being his two homes, Monticello and Poplar Forest; the Virginia State Capitol; and the core of today's University of Virginia, the aptly named "Academical Village." At his death, Jefferson bequeathed to his heirs a remarkable array of personal papers, which included drawings, correspondence, and notebooks. That, in sum, constitutes the "known."

In contrast, our understanding will forever be limited at several major works, they being the Capitol, Poplar Forest, the Rotunda at the Academical Village, and Barboursville, a fine house Jefferson designed for his friend, Governor James Barbour. In each case the structure was reduced to a mere shell by fire or, as in the case of the Capitol, by a 1904–1906 renovation. Each has virtually no original fabric aside from masonry walls. We also know little of Jefferson's earliest architectural experiences, thanks to the Shadwell fire which consumed virtually all of Jefferson's books, diaries, and other records from his first twenty-seven years.

For generations scholars have tried to understand the man, and he has been the subject of his share of both calumny and hagiography. What comes through is a long list of characteristics — everyone seems to agree he was brilliant but inconsistent; imaginative but cautious; cultured and charming but rather humorless. That very complexity is part of his appeal. But can he be characterized in a single word?

He was certainly an idealist. He wasn't particularly good at political tactics; his strategies tended to overreach. As the limited successes of his presidencies suggest, for all his greatness as a political visionary, he wasn't a very practical fellow. He was a utopian and he didn't live in the world of day-to-day matters very well. He was shy, overly sensitive to criticism, and an awful manager of money. He contradicted himself on the issue of slavery, and never came to accept the enslaved as entirely human. If he stands inordinately tall as one of the Founders, we must also recognize that, all too often, that also meant that he had his head in the clouds.

Jefferson was, in short, quirky and changeable yet also principled and idealistic. In some ways, perhaps, his buildings — especially Monticello — are emblematic of precisely that fluidity. Thus we start in the first chapter of this book by looking at his personal agrarian paradise on the hilltop Jefferson dubbed, in Italian, "little mountain."

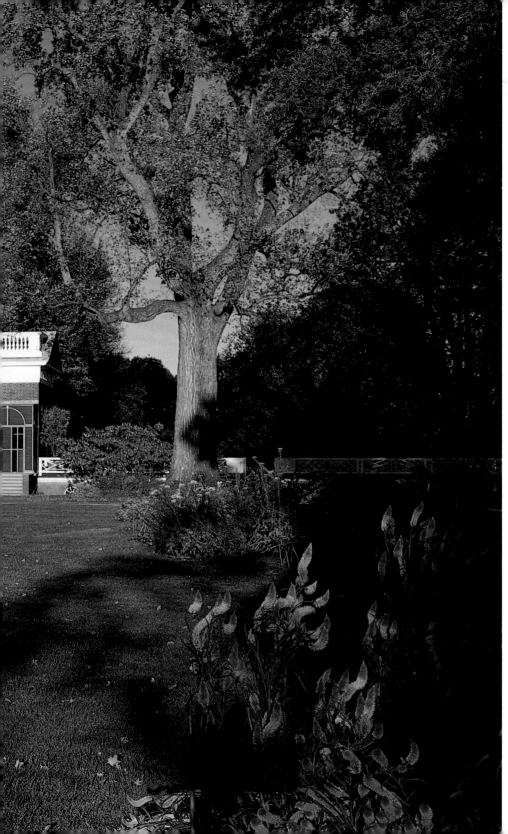

A Tale of Two Monticellos

"I am savage enough to prefer the woods, the wilds, and the independence of Monticello, to all the brilliant pleasure of this gay capital."
– Thomas Jefferson, Paris, 1785

*M*any artists over the centuries have described the moment of creation. All in a flash, they have reported, an idea leaps to mind full-blown, and they scramble to get it on paper. If the genesis of certain works of art were such epiphanies, however, Monticello is the antithesis.

Monticello is better regarded as a set of discrete yet related assays in architectural style. In a sense, it is more science than art. The house began as a paean to Palladio, a design experiment in which

The garden façade at Monticello.

Jefferson followed his master's rules and even mimicked one of his designs. For the second trial, Jefferson introduced a mix of French elements. Over a period of decades, the ever-curious Jefferson investigated and incorporated hundreds of his notions and those of others.

He revisited some ideas again and again, at Monticello and elsewhere. The octagon became a leitmotif in his domestic designs at Monticello and, as we will see later in this book, at his own retreat, Poplar Forest, as well as at Barboursville and Farmington, homes that he designed for friends. As usual, the octagon was not a Jefferson invention – one of his favorite sources, *Select Architecture* by Roger Morris, featured numerous examples – but he halved and stuck squares in them to suit his own purposes. He played with columned porticos, triple-hung sash, the de l'Orme dome, English notions of pleasure gardens, skylights, metal roof surfaces, and all manner of other architectural contrivances.

To tell the tale of Monticello is to revisit much of Jefferson's adult life; the stories of the man and his house are long, complex, and inseparable. He began to build his home in his middle twenties before 1770; the parged brick columns that finished the west portico were put in place three years before his death in 1826. The construction of Monticello consumed much of his energies – and energized him – off and on for some *fifty-four* years. Foundation work and brickmaking began when Jefferson was a tall and imposing red-haired twenty-six-year old; when the workers finally completed the façades in 1823, the man who watched them depart was a gray and slightly stooped eighty years of age.

As the title of this chapter suggests, Monticello actually had two manifestations and, as has become standard in the Jefferson literature, reference will be made in these pages to "Monticello I" and "Monticello II" in order to distinguish them. The first was a house conceived by a young man before the American Revolution and brought to near completion as that war ended. After a decade's hiatus, work on Monticello II began, a complete redesign for a sadder, more worldly widower.

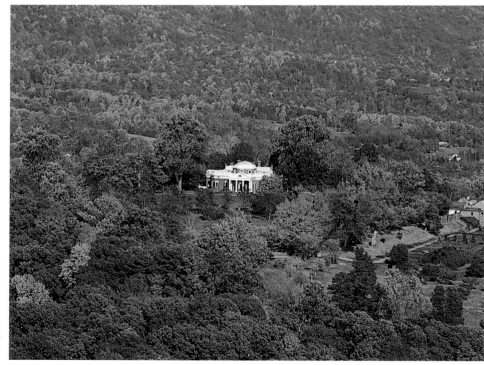

The view from above – that is, from a taller hill nearby – suggests the splendid isolation of Monticello.

Another quarter century was required to complete the remodeling. Along the way, Thomas Jefferson, Architect, completed one of the most remarkable architectural apprenticeships of all time.

As the story goes – and it was recounted many times by Jefferson himself – Thomas and Martha Wayles Jefferson arrived at Monticello in one of the biggest snow storms ever recorded in Albemarle County. Married on New Year's Day, 1772, they had then embarked on a wedding trip, visiting such imposing homes as Shirley (where Jefferson's carriage had to be repaired) and Tuckahoe, the plantation where the groom had spent most of his early childhood. The last leg of the journey took them on horseback and on foot some eight miles through more than two and even three feet of snow. The couple arrived late at night to find the servants had all retired to their quarters leaving no welcoming fire. According to family lore, they did discover a bottle of wine hidden on a bookshelf and they closed the evening with "song, merriment, and laughter."

Their destination that night was not the mansion we know today. That large and commodious home was decades in the future and, sadly, Martha wouldn't live to see it. On that snowy night late in January, the newlyweds were ensconced in a modest eighteen-foot square house, with a kitchen below and an all-purpose space for dining, entertaining, working, and sleeping above.

The so-called Honeymoon Cottage was, in an eighteenth-century sense, a starter house. Not only was it their first home together, but the brick structure had also been Thomas Jefferson's architectural practicum. Work on the hilltop had been underway for several years. Jefferson's *Garden Books* and *Farm Books* record the planting of an orchard, the milling of chestnut boards, the dig-

This is Jefferson's vision of Monticello just as he dreamt it – and then drew it – probably during the winter of 1770-1771. Courtesy of the Massachusetts Historical Society.

In its final incarnation, Jefferson's study – he called it his cabinet *– became a kind of architectural thinking cap, filled as it was with his desk, polygraph, telescope, books, and innumerable contraptions. He needed solitude and at most of his residences – not only at Monticello, but at Poplar Forest, in his Philadelphia domicile, and even in Paris – he established such private spaces where he could be alone with his books, his papers, and his thoughts.*

ging of a foundation, the making of brick, and the purchase of glass and hardware. He had long planned to move there, but the cottage became Jefferson's bachelor quarters by November of 1770, after his family home at Shadwell had been consumed by flames.

The Cottage still stands, though today it is simply a pavilion at one extreme of Monticello. The contrast between the modest brick cube and the sprawling complex of the mansion and its dependencies is instructive.

At Monticello I, the dining room was the first room in the main house to be completed. Clearly that was no accident: With the exception of reading, lingering at table was Jefferson's favorite pastime. Throughout his life, he recorded recipes in his notebooks. Wine, as well, was one of his pleasures, and he tried to establish a vineyard at Monticello (though he failed at wine-making, his cellar was usually well stocked with European vintages he could ill afford).

Dining was a social experience at Monticello (as well as at his homes-away-from-home, including the President's House in Washington and the Hôtel de Langeac in Paris). A meal taken in Jefferson's company was an intellectual experience, as well, where ideas and amusements and pleasantries were to be exchanged. As a politician, he more often conducted his business at table than anyplace else.

In this image, note the opening in the side of the mantelpiece – it reveals a dumbwaiter that delivered wine from the cellar below.

Jefferson's vision expanded over the years, his tastes grew more eclectic, and the decades saw a great deal of construction (and demolition). But the first building was clearly a rite of passage for its builder. An architect isn't truly an architect until he or she builds something, until the act of imagination that produces a design on paper is translated into the physical action of construction. For Jefferson, the rising from the earth of that life-size, three-dimensional building constituted his first architectural endeavor. And the cold and dark accommodation

This is the south terrace, looking toward Jefferson's private quarters; camouflaged beneath this boardwalk are the dependencies. At other plantations of the time, separate, purpose-built structures for the kitchen and stable areas were freestanding, but at Monticello Jefferson integrated them into the house complex.

that he and Martha found that night presaged something of the character of their ten years together living in what was effectively a construction site.

Imagine the Jeffersons' pavilion quarters. No doubt the place was aclutter with books and furniture, together with objects the curious and acquisitive Jefferson had accumulated. The view from the window to the east was of the building site where a much more ambitious house would stand. To the north, recent excavation had flattened the hill-top, a first step in establishing a manicured pleasure garden. But the eye would certainly be drawn beyond the immediate area to a larger and grander landscape. From Jefferson's hilltop there was – and is – a panoramic vista of the central Virginia countryside.

This was not your average building site. In the eighteenth century, people rarely built houses on hilltops. Virginia planters typically built on the James or other rivers for ease of transport of crops and other goods. Delivering food, building materials, and even people to the top of Monticello at 867 feet altitude would have been a

On this floor plan of both Monticellos, the cross-hatching around the rooms to the rear (Jefferson's bedroom, the parlor, and the dining room) indicates the perimeter of Monticello I, which was subsumed by the larger and later version of the house. Monticello/Thomas Jefferson Foundation.

daunting prospect. But Jefferson, dreamer and idealist, had crisscrossed his properties on horseback countless times and he knew the site he wanted. He had known it for years, his daughter Martha reported later ("I have heard my father say that when quite a boy the top of this mountain was his favorite retreat . . . and that the indescribable delight he here enjoyed so attached him to this spot, that he determined when arrived at manhood he would here build his family mansion."

Perhaps he also took his cue from Palladio who recommended villas be built in "elevated and agreeable places." We know Palladio did not have in mind a site like Jefferson's "little mountain" – the topography of Palladio's native Veneto features fewer and smaller hills – but Jefferson knew Palladio's *terra firma* only from books. Jefferson's choice of site really wasn't a practical one, as the hilltop wells repeatedly went dry. Yet siting Monticello where he did was just one of a thousand decisions Jefferson made that distinguish the individuality of his vision.

Somewhere in that cottage were Jefferson's architectural plans, perhaps all in a roll tied with a string. Jefferson had watched his father at his drafting table and, at Peter Jefferson's death, had inherited his surveying instruments. By

The so-called "nickel façade," the face of Monticello that overlooks Mr. Jefferson's gardens.

1772, the younger Jefferson had begun to master the craft of architectural drawing, and even today more than two dozen studies survive from the years preceding his marriage. There are plans of the site as well as the house and its foundation. There are studies of garden buildings, elevations, and even a few working drawings. An overall scheme had emerged for the arrangement of the house and "dependencies" that in substance, though not in detail, would endure to this day.

The house itself was to consist of three parts. At the center would be a tall, gable-roofed structure with porticoes on the opposite façades, one for entry and the other facing the garden. On either side of the central block would be two shorter, hip-roofed wings. The ground floor of the central block would contain the entrance hall and main parlor, with a dining room in the north wing and the master's bedroom to the south. Though its scale was generous, this was not a large house with four rooms down and one upstairs. But it was part of a larger plan which included two, matching *L*-shaped service wings that were to extend out and connect to the Honeymoon Cottage and a mirror image pavilion on the opposite side of the garden. The garden the service buildings embraced would be 250 feet wide.

This plan was probably amended at the time Martha Wayles Skelton married Thomas Jefferson. Additional rooms, semi-octagonal in shape, were added to each wing of the house. By far the largest private room had been the library, but Mrs. Jefferson would have seen the need for more family space (she was with child within days of their marriage). Her concerns no doubt figured into the planning, but we have little sense of the give and take of their rela-

The parlor features French furniture Jefferson acquired on his travels abroad, including Louis XVI chairs and a marble pedestal table called a guéridon.

tionship since Jefferson destroyed their correspondence at her death and, as the years passed, increasingly idealized her memory. Since the practice of the time was to give over domestic management to the lady of the house, we can reasonably conclude she helped shape the plan for the dependencies.

Monticello was never conceived as simply a dwelling. Like the villas Palladio designed for the Veneto, Monticello was to be a grand country house *and* an administrative center for a large working farm which, in colonial Virginia, was worked by hundreds of slaves. In designing a number of his most memorable villas, Palladio had planted the house at the center, and flanked it with long barn buildings called *barchesse*. At each end he set other farm buildings, typically dovecotes which were effectively chicken houses.

The Jeffersonian variation from the Palladian paradigm was to place the miscellaneous buildings, the "dependencies," below grade. This gave the central block more prominence and obscured the sight and sounds of the work of the house. The large scale work of the farm was done at satellite farms closer to the fields in tillage, but Jefferson rationalized into the careful plan of his immediate domicile many activities that on other Virginia plantations had evolved into a more haphazard array of outbuildings. His south dependencies would contain the kitchen, pantry, and spaces for brewing beer, smoking meats, and processing dairy products. To the north of the house were to be stables and a carriage house. The house and dependencies constituted a self-contained community.

Jefferson designed Monticello himself, but that isn't to say he worked entirely alone. In addition to contributions from his wife, the plan drew upon several published sources. One was almost certainly *Select Architecture* by Robert

From the garden (facing page) Monticello's defining characteristic is its dome. Ironically, on the inside the "sky room," as Jefferson called it, proved to be almost unusable because of the difficulty in reaching it on staircases that were a mere two feet wide (Jefferson observed ". . . great stair cases are avoided, which are expensive and occupy a space which would make a good room in every story"). So Jefferson's grand octagonal room with its fashionable grass-green floor was used as a children's playroom.

The structure of the dome was based in part on one he saw in France at the Halle aux Bleds made after the design of Philibert de l'Orme. It was not of stone but of wood, with lengths of lumber cut into short segments of an arc then overlapped and laminated to form the ribs of the dome. The design was efficient, affordable, within the skills of the workers available, and it utilized native materials (wood was at hand, cut stone was not). The dome at Monticello also proved to be a study for the larger one later raised over the Rotunda at the University of Virginia.

Morris, as there's a surviving floor plan in Jefferson's own hand traced from one of the plates in *Select Architecture*. Jefferson also worked from James Gibbs' *Rules for Drawing the Several Parts of Architecture*. A third source, not surprisingly, was Palladio, with the two-story stacks of columns that defined the porticoes on the east and west façades bearing no small resemblance to Palladio's Villa Cornaro.

Jefferson was self-consciously working in a grand tradition. The goal was, in an eighteenth-century sense, imitation. That did not imply precise copying but, as the poet John Dryden had written, "In the way of imitation, the translator not only varies from the words and sense, but forsakes them as he sees occasion . . . taking only some general hints from the original . . . ." Jefferson translated what he saw in Palladio, Morris, Gibbs, and others, using what he liked but not slavishly. For example, in Roman and Renaissance times, a pediment was a sign of rank, often decorated with a carved coat of arms. But Jefferson skipped over the status symbol coat of arms and inserted a lunette window instead. His use of half-round lunette windows in the recessed surface of the triangular tympanum in a pediment (an echo of windows in Roman baths) became a characteristic Jefferson touch.

In that pre-industrial age, much had to be done by hand, so building progressed at a very deliberate pace. Many people grew accustomed to living in houses that were incomplete for sustained periods, but Monticello was an extreme case. For the ten-plus years of her marriage to Thomas Jefferson, Martha's home was a work in progress. The first rooms in the north wing of the main house, a dining room below and bedroom above, were probably in use by 1773. Jefferson moved his books into the house that year, too, but it wasn't to the second floor library since that remained unfinished. Staging for masons and carpenters came and went with the seasons inside the house and out. And Jefferson did the same, departing for months at a time as a member of the Continental Congress and the Virginia House of Delegates. In his absence, work usually stopped.

Since Jefferson distrusted wood for enclosing a house and stone simply wasn't an option (there was no suitable native stone in Virginia and importing it would have been prohibitively expensive), bricks were made on site by molding, stacking, and then firing them for several days in a "clamp," a self-contained kiln. The woodwork was sawn and shaped from trees felled on nearby acreage of Jefferson's. The mountain top, then, was filled with smoke, sawdust, noise, and activity. Though it had yet to be invented, Martha Jefferson deserved an honorary hard hat for her willingness to weave her way between brick clamps, lumber piles, staging platforms, a small army of workers – *and*, while doing so, producing a child every other year. When Jefferson departed to assume the Virginia governorship in Williamsburg in 1779, the house was probably "finished" to the degree that all of its rooms were habitable, but even five years later, when Jefferson departed to become minister to France, few of the architectural details were in place.

The first incarnation of Monticello (1769-1782) should be thought of as a somewhat mythical building. The house as Jefferson conceived it was never fully realized, the building process so prolonged that it outlasted his marriage. A private man who wrote only rarely of his emotional life, Jefferson usually contented himself with thoughts of "the consolations of a sound philosophy, equally indifferent to hope and fear." But sweet reason offered little solace when Martha Wayles Jefferson died in September 1782, a few months before what would have been their eleventh wedding anniversary.

In the wake of his wife's death, Jefferson was beyond consolation. According to contemporary accounts, he was so stricken with grief that he was unable to speak or even to see his children without swooning. Some six weeks

These dependencies, which include the kitchen, spaces for food processing and storage, and slave quarters, were invisible from the pleasure garden above because they were built into the slope of the hill. Yet on the downhill side there was light and ventilation.

after Martha's death he recovered enough to seek comfort in the company of her namesake, their eldest daughter, Martha, who had recently turned ten years of age. They took long rides together that she later remembered as "melancholy rambles."

Returning to Monticello from such rides could only have reminded him of the terrible emptiness he felt. When Martha Jefferson died, the house was little more than a solidly built masonry envelope, a dwelling as incomplete as his life had become. The mass of the main house stood tall and the walls within were plastered. But the porticos were only half completed, the dependencies no more than paper plans. Although Jefferson would half-heartedly revise a standing order for columns and other architectural ornamentation the following year, construction at Monticello was effectively halted the day Jefferson became a widower.

Monticello I survives in a few drawings, most memorably in an elevation drawing, an orthographic projection that represents the front façade as it would have appeared to an observer looking at it from a horizontal vantage (see page 29). Building fabric exists from Monticello I, but it is about as distinguishable as the rusted hulk of a 30s automobile after a 50s hot rodder had chopped and channeled it into a street rod. The original, half-finished Monticello was swallowed up by later versions, both the larger, more sophisticated house Jefferson would devise in the next decade and the monumental work that stands today, the work of subsequent restorers. The first Monticello, like a half-finished water color left out in the rain, gradually faded into memory.

Despite its incompleteness and subsequent disappearance, however, the lost Monticello was no failed experiment. What we know of Monticello I offers many clues as to the evolution of Jefferson's architectural imagination. A simple three-part house gained angularity with the addition of the semi-octagons. In the drawings the hand of the draftsman grows noticeably more confident, more skilled. The house provided him an early trial with classical orders, an opportunity to impose a Renaissance skin on colonial bones. If Monticello I was derivative and boxy, then it reflected the unease and inexperience of its designer. It was an interrupted dream – and Monticello II would be a different house indeed.

The man who designed the first Monticello knew little of the world first-hand. When he took the five-day horseback ride to William and Mary College as a sixteen-year-old, he traveled 100 miles. That was a distance several times as great as any he had traveled before from his childhood home at Shadwell. He was twenty-three when he visited Philadelphia and New York to obtain a smallpox vaccination. That brief 1766 trip constituted the entire extent of his travels beyond the borders of Virginia prior to designing Monticello.

A generation later, however, when he embarked upon the remodeling of Monticello, Jefferson had lived for extended periods in Philadelphia, the wealthiest American city in the years after independence. He had also resided in Annapolis, among the most stylish American cities of the colonial period. He had traveled through New England, portions of New York, and, most important of all, he had spent five years in Europe, based in Paris.

As Minister to France he had taken advantage of a diplomatic mission to England in 1786 to tour great landscape gardens. He and John Adams made dozens of stops at notable eighteenth-century sites, including the palaces at Windsor and Blenheim and the great houses and pleasure gardens at Chiswick and Stowe. The following year on doctor's orders (his broken right wrist from the previous September had healed poorly), he managed an extended tour to the south of France and northern Italy. He spent nearly fifteen weeks tirelessly visiting dozens of towns and cities and sites. He rarely stopped for more than one night, and saw Nice, Lyons, and Aix-en-Provence before crossing the Alps to visit Turin, Milan, and Genoa. He got to see the Maison Carrée, the building that inspired his design of Virginia's Capitol, a commission he carried out while abroad (see Chapter 2, "A New Capitol for the Commonwealth," page 63). In 1788, a third European detour took him to Amsterdam to complete arrangements for a large loan to the United States, and he traveled through parts of Germany and the Netherlands.

His tour of duty (1784-1789) as Minister was Jefferson's chance to be a Grand Tourist, but of all the places he saw Paris left the deepest impression. He found the place congenial, its people, salons, galleries, book shops, and gardens sophisticated and stimulating. Jefferson immediately found old buildings to admire, and the city itself was a virtual construction site, with the visionary architects Ledoux and Boullée bringing a fresh slant to classical antiquity. Jefferson rented himself a house, the Hôtel de Langeac, and, as was always his way, he shortly commenced renovating. Other buildings found places in his architectural imagination, especially an in-town house under construction, the Hôtel de Salm, with which Jefferson found himself "violently smitten." A grand private home with a central dome, the Hôtel de Salm proved

The "Indian Hall," as the entry was also known, was filled with Jefferson's collections, ranging from maps and moose antlers to a marble of Ariadne. There were Indian artifacts, too, as that's a Mandan buffalo robe hanging over the mezzanine railing (below).

Like the entry halls at other great houses, the Indian Hall was used to screen the many people who came to see the man of the house. But Jefferson, himself a lifelong learner, couldn't resist the opportunity to offer his visitors edification. These objects were an expression of his wealth and wisdom, but also a democratic sharing of what he knew. And there is an element of patriotism here, too, as Jefferson often expressed his pride at the natural beauty, scale, and possibility of America. In fact, the contents here speak for the complexity of Jefferson. He admired the classical in its ancient, renaissance, and contemporary expressions; he was a champion of things American (he found the Indian noble, even if the African never earned such status in his eyes); and he bragged to Europeans about the size of America and its natural life (thus the mastodon bones and the elk rack).

The terraces on the southeastern side of Monticello provided Jefferson the horticulturist a living laboratory for his experiments. He grew some seventy species of vegetables in the main garden, while a range of fruit trees and grape vines descended the hillside. At the focus he set his pavilion, capped with its Chinese railing, a place where he could find quiet apart from the bustle of the little village that was his mountaintop home. Though destroyed in the nineteenth century, the pavilion was reconstructed in 1984 on the basis of archaeological findings and Jefferson's notes.

to be the single most significant inspiration for his reinvention of Monticello, just as a plate in Palladio's *Four Books* had been for Monticello I. He borrowed both the dome and the Hôtel's clever two-stories-disguised-as-one design.

If Jefferson broadened the foundations of his architectural knowledge on his Parisian sojourn, he also regained his emotional equilibrium during his time abroad. While in Paris, the widower Jefferson was deeply captivated by a beautiful woman named Maria Cosway. Born in Italy of English parents, the flaxen-haired Cosway was cultured, worldly, and a talented artist in her own right. She had a husband, a miniaturist named Richard Cosway, but her marriage may have been one of convenience.

The nature of Jefferson's liaison with Maria Cosway can never be known, despite the survival of much correspondence and the efforts of so many scholars and even filmmakers (*Jefferson in Paris*) to explicate their affair. But his passion for Maria Cosway – it was at least an infatuation, whether consummated or not – certainly provided an emotional catharsis. As he strove to understand his own affections, he resorted to pen and paper and wrote her the so-called "head-and-heart" letter, the most famous missive in a long letter-writing life. In that letter he speculated on the relative powers of intellect and emotion, casting his head and heart as voices in a dialogue. The letter, some

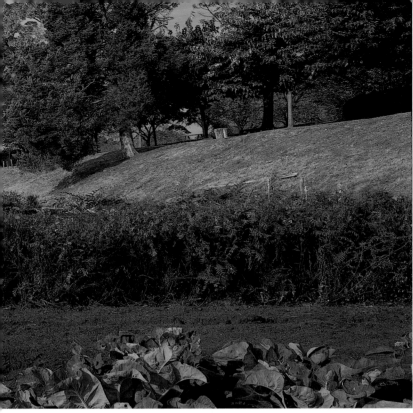

4,000 words long, finds him poised, moving from one phase of his life to another. This dalliance and the presumed intimacy he shared with Maria Cosway didn't change the direction of Jefferson's life. On the other hand, the half-life of that half-love may have been just the stimulus he needed to move on, to take even greater advantage of his time abroad. And it got him thinking of Monticello again as he described it to Maria Cosway.

Jefferson's Parisian time required that he look up and around himself. He set the sadness of his wife's death aside during this one great hiatus from his American life. As he sailed home to America in the autumn of 1789, he brought back his share of souvenirs, some *eighty* crates of furniture and other goods. Perhaps during the Atlantic crossing he cogitated upon the changes he would make to his unfinished home but, upon stepping off the ship in Norfolk on November 23rd, he learned that Congress had confirmed his nomination as Secretary of State in the Washington administration. Several more years would pass before he would be free to return to private life.

His time abroad had effected a transformation. The well-read country lad had become a man of the world. Thomas Jefferson,

Note the "porticles" or "Venetian enclosures" that flank this, the south wing of Monticello. Jefferson put them there for privacy, to keep people from peering into his quarters. The closer corner porticle was constructed by John Hemings as an aviary, probably for mockingbirds.

Architect, was no longer so reliant on his book learning but developed notions in his own mind, as visions of real buildings coalesced with the plates in his library. He had already built the first version of his house, designed a capitol in 1785-86, and in the coming years would confidently engage in designing other peoples' homes (see Chapter 3, "Dwellings for Friends and Family," page 85). As his days as Secretary of State waned, he wrote to a friend that he wanted very much "to be liberated from the hated occupation of politics, and to remain in the bosom of my family, my farm, and my books."

And, he added, "I have my house to build."

From Jefferson's private quarters he had easy access to this terrace walkway – and a broad vista of the Virginia countryside.

❖

Jefferson returned to Charlottesville prepared to reinvent his house. He would more than double its footprint, adding a second, parallel row of rooms along the north-south axis of the original five-room plan. Among these new spaces would be an entry hall, service corridors, more bedrooms, and a first-floor library. The height of the building would change, too. Jefferson planned to lower the porticos, eliminating the second level of columns. Following a contemporary French convention, the second floor windows would also be lowered. Skylights would be added to the roof, hidden by

From the entry Hall, a visitor to Monticello would have moved into the Parlor, its walls lined with paintings. Among other objects in the room were a Houdon bust of Jefferson, a harpsichord that daughter Martha often played for guests, and a siesta or "campeachy" chair. Probably made by John Hemings, this semi-reclining chair was a comfort to Jefferson when he suffered one of his periodic bouts of rheumatism.

a railing lining the roof perimeter. The result would be the appearance of a gracious, one-story house, but with three levels of living space, including the ground floor, a mezzanine, and an attic. The top level would also feature the dome room, an octagonal space with a hemispherical ceiling inspired by Palladio's Roman researches but built in accordance with contemporary French construction practices.

Upon Jefferson's retirement to private life in 1793, he was able to devote substantial time and energy to developing this plan and to accumulating materials. The remodeling of Monticello also required demolishing a good deal of the original structure. The front portico was dismantled. The entire roof of the house had to come off, too, and the walls of the upper story lowered. The demolition began in 1794 and continued until 1796 when reconstruction began. Even though Jefferson was running for president that year, his candidacy didn't interfere with progress as he never left Monticello during the campaign. He lost the election, but as runner up he became vice president to John Adams. Then the work at Monticello slowed once again.

When his daughter Maria was married in October 1797 the house remained very much a work site. The discrete sections of the main block roof and those atop the two flanking wings had allowed portions of the house to be dismantled, rebuilt, and reroofed separately. But it wasn't until the first year of the new century that a new roof covered the entire building. Progress was threatened again when, in February 1801, the disputed presidential election of the previous year was resolved in the House of Representatives in Jefferson's favor (on the thirty-sixth bal-

From the Parlor, an honored guest might be invited into the Dining Room, where a meal of the sort for which Jefferson was famous might be served, with food prepared with fresh ingredients from his expansive gardens according to recipes his enslaved chef had learned in France. In this photograph, the dining furniture is "at rest," having been moved to the periphery of the room, as was done after meals.

lot, he prevailed over Aaron Burr). But by this time Jefferson had finally found a workman he could trust to oversee construction in his absence.

Irishman James Dinsmore was a master carpenter Jefferson had hired in Philadelphia in 1798. Jefferson bought him tools which he had shipped directly to Monticello. Dinsmore would remain at Monticello for ten years, doing much of the interior work on the house, as well as working for extended periods producing windows and other millwork for Jefferson's second home, Poplar Forest (see Chapter 4, "An Escape to Poplar Forest," page 115). He seems to have been the key player in a platoon of proven craftsmen that Jefferson felt he could command from his residence in the new President's House in the new capital of Washington, D.C. The dependencies – the kitchen wing to the south, the stable wing to the north – were finally begun, almost thirty years after Thomas and Martha had first planned them.

On Jefferson's visits home, he could see real progress. In an 1802 watercolor painted by Anna Maria Thornton the garden façade looks virtually finished, with the roof parapets in place. The dome, begun by Dinsmore in 1800, had the oculus window at its acme, a four-and-a-half foot sheet of glass, put in place in 1805. The interior of the house was nearly completed when Jefferson retired from the presidency, since we know a master painter from

The Tea Room at Monticello with its of busts of worthies, including Benjamin Franklin and George Washington.

Washington, Richard Barry, came and went between 1805 and 1808, spending roughly two years painting the interior. In February of 1809 Dinsmore installed some final pieces of cornice molding before taking his leave to work on James Madison's nearby home, Montpelier.

Among other key workers from that decade are John Neilson, Hugh Chisholm, John Perry, and John Hemings. Neilson was another Ulsterman whom Jefferson hired in Philadelphia. He and Dinsmore were in Jefferson's words, "house jointers of the first order." Neilson was perhaps the most learned of Jefferson's builders, leaving at his death in 1827 a substantial library. His 248 books were devoted to a range of subjects worthy of Jefferson (botany, history, travel, mathematics, and, of course, architecture). He owned carpentry and gardening tools, as well as drawing utensils, and a number of his drawings of Jefferson projects survived.

Carpenter-joiner James Oldham not only worked for Jefferson on Monticello but in 1804 Oldham borrowed one of Jefferson's personal copies of the first volume of Palladio's *Four Books*. Hugh Chisholm was another long time retainer of Jefferson's; he was a mason, while John Perry did framing. Many of these men went on to work for friends of Jefferson's (see especially Bremo and Estouteville, pages 172 and 175, respectively), only to return to his employ once again when work at the University of Virginia commenced in 1817. After his death, some of them lived on and continued to spread the gospel according to Jefferson.

In mastering any skill, there's a learning curve to be surmounted. At the beginning there are false starts and moments of fumbling. Over time, the process becomes familiar and easier; there are fewer rude surprises and confidence grows. The modest person will admit that mastery is a relative concept. Even after decades, great chess players, artists, and students of human nature gain new understandings each day. Yet there is a point at which there's a new fluidity and an ability to anticipate the next step. The command of the materials is suddenly there, the grasp of the business at hand newly assured.

One can only guess as to when Thomas Jefferson, Architect, felt fully in the flow but he must have been buoyed by the momentum – and perhaps a sense of mastery – in the last years of his presidency. His beloved Monticello rapidly advanced toward completion. John Neilson and James Dinsmore were doing finish work while John Perry was framing and surfacing the roof of the house and the terraces over the dependencies. Hugh Chisolm was plastering and raising chimneys.

The first floor of the south wing is essentially a one-man men's club, including a vast library, an indoor-outdoor piazza space that contained his workbench and greenhouse (opposite page); and his most personal space, the cabinet (below), and his bedroom (right). Note the triple-hung sash in the bedroom, a favorite design element of Jefferson's that contributed light, height, and ventilation.

By the time Jefferson came home after James Madison's inauguration in March of 1809, Monticello was virtually finished. The former president retired to a dream largely realized forty years after construction had begun.

When Jefferson bade farewell to most of his skilled workers, he wasn't left without artisans at hand to call upon for various work about the place. He would never stop revising Monticello, and nothing was predictable about the work there except that the pace would be irregular and its owner's restless intelligence would always be at play. But he increasingly relied upon John Hemings and men like Burwell and Lewis, two skilled workers who are remembered by one name each. When work began at Monticello, all of Jefferson's skilled workers had been free men but by 1809 Jefferson's *Farm Book* listed Hemings, Burwell, Lewis and nineteen other slaves trained in carpentry, masonry, blacksmithing, and other trades.

Though enslaved, John Hemings was the son of an early Monticello worker, Joseph Neilson, and had apprenticed with James Dinsmore. He had become a superb craftsman whose workmanship helped shape not only

Charleston, South Carolina, native Robert Mills was the first American-born and American-trained architect. He was a pupil of two immigrant architects (Englishman Benjamin Latrobe and the Irish designer of the president's house, James Hoban) as well as of Jefferson. This circa 1803 rendering of the west elevation of Monticello was drawn during his time at Monticello and it portrays the west elevation as built.
Courtesy of the Massachusetts Historical Society.

Monticello but Poplar Forest. He and Lewis produced much furniture in the Monticello cabinet shop, sometimes in collaboration with Jefferson himself. Lewis had apprenticed with the other Neilson, the talented Irisher, John. Richard Barry had trained Burwell, Jefferson's personal servant, to become Monticello's resident painter.

Monticello could not have been built without slave labor. Slaves did much of the unskilled work, excavating the site and moving, hauling, and fabricating raw materials like bricks, lumber, and nails. Throughout the building campaigns slaves were apprenticed to white craftsman because Jefferson couldn't afford to pay for a full crew of freemen to do the work. The money simply wasn't in his coffers, and as it was he overspent wildly. Just weeks before his death friends sold tickets for a lottery, the proceeds of which were to go to the payment of Jefferson's overdue bills. This pathetic scheme, like most financial gambits associated with Jefferson, was a failure.

While it is not within the purview of this book to render any Solomonic judgements about Jefferson's slaveholding, the brutal facts are that Jefferson owned hundreds of slaves, some inherited, some born to slaves he owned, still others bought and sold. They farmed his lands, cooked his food, nursed his children, and performed countless other tasks. The headline name, of course, is Sally Hemings. She was John's sister, a member of a talented family of cooks, servants, and craftsmen that Jefferson had inherited on the death of his father-in-law, John Wayles, in 1773. Along with her mother, Betty, Sally had taken part in the death watch at Martha Wayles Jefferson's bedside. She witnessed the promise that Martha extracted from her husband never to remarry, a promise he honored. Bonds of intimacy and interdependence were common between slave owners and their household slaves, but in the case of the Wayles family and, later, the Jeffersons, the connections reached deeply into the gene pool. Sally was Martha Wayles' half-sister, the daughter of John Wayles (who himself had been a slave trader). In 1786, fourteen-year-old Sally would be entrusted with the care of Jefferson's younger daughter, Maria, on her trans-Atlantic voyage to join Jefferson in Paris. Later Jefferson — according to generations of oral history in the Hemings' family as well as recent DNA evidence — would father several of Sally's children.

This is inflammatory but unavoidable territory. In our time, any position on slavery but condemnation is unconscionable. Early in his life Jefferson had expressed his opposition to the ownership of other humans but his youthful protestations later gave way to tacit approval. While Jefferson had been essential to freeing white Americans from bondage to an English king, slavery proved a pernicious custom he was unable to throw off. He owned slaves his entire adult life and freed only five in his will, including the devoted manservant Burwell, John Hemings, and two of Sally's children, Eston and Madison. Sally was not on the list.

Jefferson's memory has been tarnished both by his slaveholding and his inability to balance his books. It's well known he died a debtor, leaving his beloved heirs financial obligations that required two generations to clear. But if he had lived within his means, Monticello would have remained nothing more than the proverbial glint in its creator's eye, an impossible dream, unaffordable, unrealizable. But Jefferson lived by a different code, distracted both by the minutiae of his ledgers (with countless columns of figures he never footed) and a vision of something out of most people's sight. He ranged far and wide over vast intellectual territories, while living by an unwise fiscal philosophy, one that cannot be separated from slavery. He needed money to fulfill his dreams, and no doubt he rather wished slavery would go away. But in a life characterized by bright ideas and good works, even Thomas Jefferson didn't know how to reinvent that part of the system. The passage of decades, the appearance on the scene of other men with a lesser stake in the status quo, and a horrifying war would be required to make that leap.

Jefferson blended traditional style with a miscellany of the newest conveniences. One of his favorite innovations was the alcove bed, which he used not only in his own home but also recommended to his friends. In his bedroom he used the storage area above the bed as a closet for off-season clothing. The ports are for ventilation.

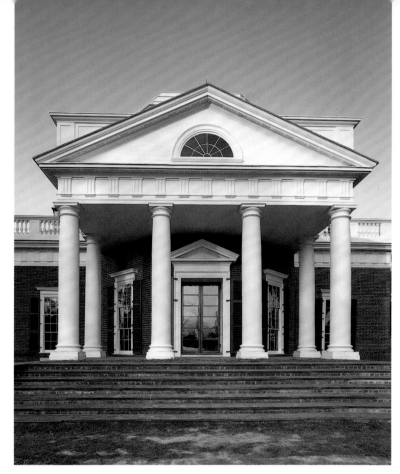

As with his later buildings at the University of Virginia, Monticello features specimens of good taste in architecture. The portico on the garden façade is a case in point. It's textbook Doric, with its bold columns and an entablature lined with triglyphs, the raised decorative blocks that suggest an ancient internal structure. Inside the house are the other orders, too. The Hall is Ionic, the Parlor Corinthian. For Jefferson, the codified system of classical ornamentation appealed not only to his artistic eye but, as a self-consciously rational man, to his sense of order.

⬦

In the years after Martha Wayles Jefferson's premature death in 1782, the programme at Monticello changed. The first house had been planned for a young couple with a growing family, but by the 1790s, Jefferson's needs were different. His penchant for entertaining had made the first plan for Monticello seem too small. Plus he had a new and more expansive domestic dream for his house: he desired very much to have his daughters, their husbands, and the prospective grandchildren around him, a tranquil and homely setting in contrast to Washington's political huggermugger.

The programme was complex and continued to evolve over many years, but the widower Jefferson was able to indulge his extraordinary obsession with the place unencumbered. Few spouses would consent to live in the chaos of a construction site for decade after decade. While Jefferson professed great love for his wife, ironically her death had allowed him to conduct his architectural experiments as if commonplace comforts such as privacy, sound roofs, and finished surfaces were of no matter. He got to build his house his way.

The eventual layout was carefully engineered to serve multiple purposes. Jefferson was famous for his hospitality, welcoming, feeding, and accommodating countless visitors over the years at Monticello. His guests walked a virtual parade route, proceeding from the museum space of the Hall into the Parlor with its display of pictures and grand view of the pleasure garden. The privileged visitor would experience not only the grandiloquence of the place but also its intimacy when served a meal in the Dining Room or the Tea Room.

Jefferson's private quarters were adjacent to yet quite apart from the public rooms. His sanctum sanctorum, or *cabinet*, adapted from a French convention of the time, had become more than a dressing room but a place to which he retired to read, write, and think. Visitors during his lifetime recalled that his private quarters were an area into which few were welcomed. He valued his privacy highly and even kept his library locked.

Jefferson indulged himself, certainly, but he was also a profoundly indulgent father, grandfather, and friend, and his dream of a busy and happy household came to be. The extended family in residence for sustained periods included his daughter Martha Jefferson Randolph, her husband, Thomas Mann Randolph, and their eleven children. Other family members and numerous guests were typically at hand, too, so the two chambers on the first floor as well as the six bedrooms on the second and three on the third were often filled.

The moment at which Thomas Jefferson, Architect, completed Monticello is subject to debate. Certainly the bulk of construction on Monticello II was accomplished in the fifteen-odd years ending in 1809 when he left the President's House for his final retirement to Charlottesville. But it wasn't until 1823 that the porticos were finally completed. By his death in 1826, however, the house, too, had aged, its roof leaking, its paint peeling. In fact, today's Monticello cannot truly represent any of the incarnations Jefferson knew. Jefferson simply never had it so good, since his finances were usually strained and he was always remaking something. Thus the house we know today, as beautiful as it is, is a painstaking reconstruction of a place with more polish than Jefferson could ever apply.

The welcoming portico at Monticello.

Monticello has become an icon, much as its builder has become larger than life. In a sense, Monticello is the quintessential American house. It's built on a hilltop – don't most Americans dream of a demesne that embraces all that they can see? It's a deeply personal house and if Jefferson believed profoundly in the dictums of classical architecture – symmetry, the orders, balance and restraint – then Monticello also manages to be idiosyncratic. It's the embodiment of the inner workings of a quirky, fast-moving mind in mid-experiment. Jefferson's architectural vision had expanded while he was abroad, as he incorporated into his design vocabulary a variety of French architectural elements, ranging from the *cabinet* with its alcove bed to the de L'Orme dome. His time in France had enabled Jefferson to loosen the hold that the rules and regulations of classicism had on him. They still applied, but he could use them more freely. Increasingly, they became decorating ideas, orders to be applied, but not dictates. He could exercise his taste for freer forms – octagonal spaces, variable ceiling heights, and especially the drama of light.

A chief joy of Monticello is the playful way in which Jefferson juggles light and space. If Frank Lloyd Wright can be accused of being heavy handed in the ways he dramatized his spaces – low, dark corridors that opened to tall vaulted spaces, for example – then Jefferson, the innocent amateur, was looking to invite his visitors to enjoy both his volumes and the majestic details he had applied. Certainly he wanted aspects of his home and other designs to educate people; yet he was also working to delight himself. If there's a sense in some of Wright's buildings that the visitor is being manipulated, at Monticello there's something fresh about Jefferson's unselfconscious attempt to illuminate, to welcome a maximum of light and air into the structure by using skylights, triple-hung sash, and semi-octagonal shapes. The contrast between Monticello as Jefferson imagined it in the 1770s and the revised edition says everything about Jefferson's evolution as an architect. If he had trouble moving beyond his books early on, then, in contrast, the chief virtue of Monticello II isn't his use of classical elements but, rather, the way he managed to use them but not be used by them. The fidelity to the esteemed sources survives but a change has taken place.

Jefferson came to understand in his experiments at Monticello that as ethereal as it is, light quite simply defines structure. That phenomenon – that light assumes form in space as it articulates structure – is at the core of the act of building. Particularly in a day when artificial illumination was poor (it's no accident that Jefferson went to bed early and rose with the sun), it is the rays of the sun that make Monticello a happy and dramatic place. He was inspired to put the house on the mountaintop; later, he opened it in new ways to the light of its wide open sky.

CHAPTER TWO

A
New Capitol
for the
Commonwealth

*"A favorable opportunity of introducing . . .
an example of architecture in the classic
style of antiquity."*
– Thomas Jefferson,
Autobiography, 1821

*C*areers can be launched in a moment.
Consider the summer day that Jefferson
received a letter from James Buchanan
and William Hay, two directors of the
Virginia board of public buildings.
Jefferson was abroad, just months into his
Paris sojourn as Minister to the French
court. The letter, dated March 20, 1785,
asked him to acquire plans for a new
Capitol building. That simple request represented both the fulfillment of an old
dream and a new opportunity. Jefferson
made the most of both.

*The Virginia State Capitol today amid
Richmond's Capitol Square.*

Since the early days of the Revolution, he had been lobbying to relocate Virginia's capital city nearer the center of the state. He believed such a move would enhance trade and serve the interests of a population that had spread continually westward. In addition, Williamsburg's tidewater climate was regarded as unhealthy, its coastal location vulnerable to military attack. Jefferson wrote his Bill for the Removal of the Seat of Government of Virginia in 1776, but it wasn't approved by the Virginia General Assembly until 1779. After becoming governor that year, he required just two days to engineer passage of the legislation that moved the Commonwealth's government to Richmond on the bank of the James River.

He had ulterior motives, too. One was his belief in the ennobling power of architecture. For Jefferson, buildings were symbolic of society, and, in the case of Virginia, the public buildings in Williamsburg represented the old ways, specifically the absolute power of the British king. The rule of King George III over the American colonies had ended and the new distribution of authority, Jefferson believed, should be reflected in its civic architecture. A decade before he

Jefferson knew that Virginia's work force lacked sophisticated carvers, so the Ionic order – which has scrolls rather than leaves on its capitals – was substituted for the Corinthian.

received the Buchanan and Hay letter, in fact, Jefferson had begun drafting plans for a new home for Virginia's elected legislature. Those surviving drawings make clear that he had in mind something quite unlike the buildings in Williamsburg that he derided as "rude, mis-shapen piles." Instead he wanted the purity of a classical temple, with porticos of freestanding columns at either end, an echo of Greek democracy and ancient Rome. Thus, the letter was a welcome invitation.

Jefferson rarely recorded his most intimate thoughts so we don't know what went through his mind when he received the missive from Messieurs Hay and Buchanan. What we do know from the historic record is that the Capitol of Virginia became his first commission, albeit one on which he collaborated both with the French antiquarian and architect Charles-Louis Clérisseau and with some unnamed and long dead Roman architect. But on that day, Jefferson began the transition from the owner-builder of a single uncompleted house to one of the most influential architects in American history.

Jefferson had already sited the new capitol during his tenure as governor, and his plat of the new town of Richmond had been incorporated into ordinances adopted on July 17, 1780. He set out buildings for each of the different branches of government, including a governor's mansion, a court house ("halls of justice"), and the Capitol, locating them in three public squares, along with a prison, public market, and executive offices in three others. The location was to be Shockhoe Hill, a ridge with a commanding view of the James River. Jefferson's plan also called for the existing community on Church Hill to be integrated into an expansive grid allowing for the city's development. With the new nation still at war, however, there were no construction monies available and the plan remained nothing more than a paperwork pipe dream.

By the time Jefferson was consulted again five years later, the proposal had been scaled down with the judicial and legislative functions consolidated into a single structure. But the arrival of the Hay-Buchanan letter could hardly have been better timed. Jefferson was visiting the Old World for the first (and only) time. Although the most adventurous of his Europeans travels were still to come (to England in 1786, the south of France and northern Italy in 1787, and to Holland and the Rhineland in 1788), he worked throughout his half-decade in Europe to acquaint himself with the classical architecture he had worshiped from afar. He had a taste for ancient and "modern" varieties, nurtured by his readings of Latin and Greek authors and his ever-increasing collection of architectural volumes. Despite his bookish familiarity, he knew he was no more than a novitiate in his chosen faith. While he would have liked to design the Capitol himself, he needed a collaborator.

"I was a considerable time before I could find an architect whose taste had been formed on a study of antient models," wrote Jefferson to Buchanan and Hay. In Charles-Louis Clérisseau (1721-1820) Jefferson found his man. Though French by birth, Clérisseau knew the ruins of ancient Rome like a native. He had spent eighteen years in Italy, having won the Prix de Rome in 1746. There he trained with Panini, who today is best remembered for his architectural fantasies or *capricci*, typically views of Roman classical monuments. Clérisseau met all the right people in his Roman days, including Piranesi and Johannes J. Winckelmann, the founder of modern archaeology.

While Clérisseau was both an artist and architect in own his right, his work as a drawing master and *cicerone* (tour guide) earned him his enduring place in architectural history. He helped train the two most important British architects of the late eighteenth century, Sir William Chambers and Robert Adam. Chambers would go on to became England's surveyor general under George III (and Chambers' writing on Chinese architecture, known to Jefferson as early as 1771, was surely an inspiration for Jefferson's "Chinese railings"). The Adamesque Style is named for Adam, together with his father and three brothers, and for more than a dozen years Robert Adam was Clérisseau's patron.

Charles-Louis Clérisseau was one of the great catalysts of his time. He played a role in the emergence of architects as a professional class, in part through his teaching but also thanks to his special mix of talents. Measured drawings of ancient buildings were necessary to study or replicate them, and in an age of revivals, his mix of artistic, archaeological, historical, and architectural expertise gave him instant standing. That Jefferson would find a man so

This side elevation of the Capitol reflects the collaboration between Jefferson and Clérisseau. The drawing, done by Jefferson on his favored gridded paper, also bears evidence of Clérisseau's presence. The latter is thought to have sketched in the brackets under some of the window sills and the inset panels over the first- and second-story windows. Courtesy of the Massachusetts Historical Society.

immersed in things classical to be a congenial mentor is hardly surprising. As Clérisseau himself later wrote to Jefferson, "The love I have for my art is such that I cannot express to you how much I have been gratified to find [in you] a true lover of antiquity."

Jefferson knew what he wanted of his capitol – at least, that is, in the abstract. He set his heart on "simple," "noble," "beautiful," "chaste," and "perfect." Those are words that represent different things to different people, but to Jefferson they all represented facets of "classical." And not French neo-classical. He didn't want something new for his Capitol, he wanted ancient classical, and he wrote persuasively to Hay and Buchanan of his rationale.

Two approaches to procuring the plans presented themselves, he advised. "[O]ne was, to leave some architect to draw an external according to his fancy, in which way, experience shews, that, about once in a thousand times, a pleasing form is hit upon; the other was, to take some model already devised, and approved by the general suffrage of the world." He had several candidates in mind, including the Erechtheum at Athens, a Roman temple at Balbec, and a third

Scale 1 square = 1'   Virginia Capitol: End elevation - Study

Though his father had been a surveyor, Jefferson was a self-taught draftsman. He worked in pen and ink as he imagined Monticello I; later, in France, he encountered the more forgiving pencil which allowed for erasures. He undoubtedly drew this front elevation of the Virginia Capitol while in Paris.

Delineator Jefferson also discovered squared paper in France. Originally produced for silk weavers, the paper had a slightly raised, scaled grid. He had little native drawing ability — his freehand renderings are charming but childish — so these tools proved valuable to him. Despite the fact he had no formal training and little innate skill, Jefferson's architectural renderings are as well executed as any eighteenth-century American drawings. Only with the arrival of European-trained designers like Benjamin Henry Latrobe was the standard raised. Courtesy of the Massachusetts Historical Society.

in Nîmes in the south of France. The last was his eventual choice. As he put it, he selected "the Maison quarrée . . . which is allowed, without contradiction, to be the most perfect and precious remain of antiquity in existence."

One of Clérisseau's credentials, a book entitled *Antiquités de la France*, played a role in their discussions. *Antiquités* is known to have been in Jefferson's library and it may have been the impetus for Jefferson to reach out to Clérisseau. The first nine plates in the 1778 book illustrated the temple about which Jefferson raved to his fellow directors back in Richmond. Thanks to Palladio, the Maison Carrée, an Augustan-era Roman Temple in Provence, already had a place on Jefferson's most-admired list, Palladio having described the circa 2-4 A.D. temple in the last of his *Four Books* (albeit in a variant form, as he adjusted it to fit his notion of perfect proportions in six woodcuts). Clérisseau must have seemed the perfect candidate. He had intimate, first-hand knowledge of the Maison Carrée having recorded it for his book. Known for his authority on classical ornamentation, he could also ensure that the proportion, orders, and other detailing on the Virginia variation would be correct.

Designing "the external" of the Capitol was only part of the job; step two would be to develop a plan for the interior. Jefferson was quick to take on that task. "As it was impossible for a foreign artist to know, what number and sizes of apartments would suit the different corps of our government . . . ," wrote Jefferson, "I undertook to form that arrangement." In short, the charge to Clérisseau became to prepare finished drawings for a building that integrated a floor plan by Jefferson into a temple closely resembling the Maison Carrée.

To facilitate construction of the Virginia Capitol, Jefferson had Clérisseau commission a precise architectural model which survives to this day. It is of plaster, reinforced with iron rods, and mounted on an oak base. The scale is 1:60 (one inch to five feet). Colonial Williamsburg Foundation/Library of Virginia.

The Capitol as it appeared, more or less, in 1830. The ocher Capitol still lacked its entry stairs at that date, and the artist added a nonexistent rectangular window in the pediment. The illustration, originally painted by William Goodacre, appeared in The History and Topography of the United States.

Carved of Carrara marble by Jean-Antoine Houdon, this statue was exe-cuted from life when Houdon traveled to Mount Vernon in the fall of 1785. Before arriving in America for installation at the Capitol, it was exhibited at the Louvre. Washington's contemporaries regarded it as an excellent likeness; said Lafayette, "That is the man himself."

The design the two men produced proved an intriguing mixture. The Capitol was to look monumental and Roman on the outside, but the single-room plan or *cella* of the Maison Carrée was ill-suited to the needs in Richmond. As a result Jefferson's plan for the interior at the Capitol isn't the least bit Roman or Athenian – in fact, it's a near relation to the Williamsburg Capitol it replaced. That building was one of those in Williamsburg he liked tolerably well (he had his criticisms of the proportions and massing, but wrote, ". . . on the whole, it is the most pleasing piece of architecture we have"). He clearly had its lay-out in mind as he drew the Richmond Capitol. Both are fronted with porticos, with the General Court just inside and a lobby or conference area between the court room in the front and the larger House of Delegates at the rear. Jefferson's monumental variation on the scheme was to raise the roof of the conference hall, creating a square, two-story space for the display of a full-length sculpture of George Washington, which Jefferson had already commissioned from Jean-Antoine Houdon. Given his fondness for skylights, it should come as no surprise that the hall was to be lit with a large one.

The exterior, too, had its variations from the original. Clérisseau lessened the depth of the portico from three to two intercolumniations to allow more light to enter the interior. Although they agreed upon the change from the Corinthian order on the Maison Carrée to the Ionic for the Capitol, Jefferson and Clérisseau apparently went rounds on which version of the Ionic to use. Finally they settled on the

Renaissance-era variety favored by Clérisseau, one that had been devised by Vincenzo Scamozzi, a pupil and collaborator of Palladio's.

While the precise nature of the give-and-take between Jefferson and Clérisseau cannot be known, we can be certain the design didn't leap fully formed from Jefferson's imagination. His experienced collaborator surely advanced the process with his suggestions. Evidence of this is a Jefferson drawing of a side elevation portraying a building quite different from the one that was built, with not one but two shallow porticos, one at each end of the building. What if, as evidence suggests, Clérisseau caused Jefferson to rethink that notion? What if it wasn't Jefferson who first broached the idea of using an extant building to copy? What if Clérisseau was the one who identified the Maison Carrée as the ideal model? If Clérisseau did all these things, does that significantly devalue Jefferson's status?

I would vote "No, not really," though Fiske Kimball's conclusion – "the Frenchman's role in the design was secondary" – seems rather peremptory. When Kimball broke the story, making the case in the *Journal of the American Institute of Architects* in 1915 that Jefferson had created the first monument of the classical revival in America, he had clearly appointed himself Jefferson's architectural campaign manager. But the nature of collaboration is that some ideas from each party are adopted, others dropped. If this were truly Clérisseau's building, it would probably look quite different; yet to diminish his considerable role would be wrong-headed. I've come to believe that given current research, the who-did-what-and-when questions are minor and, finally, moot. This successful, important, seminal building was the work of two men, both of whom made it better by their participation. But . . . bottom line? Without Jefferson this classical building would not have come to pass.

Although the cornerstone had been laid in August of the previous year, the first batches of drawings reached the directors in Richmond in 1786. Jefferson had been shocked to receive word that the foundation work on the building had begun. Tiring of their temporary quarters in a converted tobacco warehouse, some Virginia delegates had raised the possibility of moving the state government back to Williamsburg, compelling the commissioners to demonstrate progress. But the foundation they laid was larger than the footprint planned by Jefferson, requiring an increase in the proportions of the building. This was but one of a number of changes to the Jefferson-Clérisseau design.

The main block of the Capitol as rebuilt in 1904-06, with its wings and connecting hyphens.

The undertaker hired by the directors to build the Capitol, Samuel Dobie, was probably responsible for most of the alterations. Under Dobie's supervision, pilasters (flattened columns) were added, continuing the Ionic order around the perimeter of the building. The inset panels between the windows lost their garlands. The low pedestal base Jefferson had imagined was replaced by a tall basement, which added needed floor space (Jefferson, perhaps unrealistically, had located offices in the attic). The grand, full-width stairs to the portico of the Jefferson-Clérisseau design were omitted, allowing for front windows and a central door on the basement level.

Though he exercised no control over construction (he was in Paris as Minister and then in Philadelphia as Secretary of State), the Capitol progressed in the Jefferson manner: it took more than twelve years to complete the building. When the General Assembly managed to convene its first session in its new home in October 1788, the portico, interior, and even roof remained unfinished. The brick shafts of the columns were completed in 1789, the portico the following year. The Houdon statue of George Washington made its belated arrival in 1796, having been stored for years in the artist's studio awaiting the completion of the hall interior. By 1796, as well, the exterior cornice was finished, but it was late in 1797 before window architraves, Ionic capitals, and a coat of stucco were added. The Capitol reached substantial completion only in 1798.

Even before it was finished, admiring remarks were being made about the Capitol. The duc de La Rochefoucault-Liancourt certainly approved when he visited in 1796. In his book *Voyage dans les États Unis d'Amérique* he wrote that "in its present unfinished state, this building is, beyond comparison, the first, the most noble, and the greatest in all America." Even allowing for a bit of self-congratulation – the duc recognized the Capitol had been based upon the Maison Carrée – his high praise was no doubt welcome indeed.

The building we see today differs in notable ways from its original appearance. In 1861, it became the Capitol of the Confederacy and, fortunately, was essentially unharmed by the conflict. Yet by the close of the Civil War a lack of maintenance had left the structure in poor condition. As early as the 1830s sagging joists were noted in the upper floors and, in the 1850s, more warning signs had been detected. Little was done, however, and in 1870 the overloaded gallery in a second story courtroom crashed to the floor which, in turn, collapsed into the Hall of Delegates below.

Even the deaths of sixty-two people in what came to be known as the "Capitol Disaster" weren't sufficient to galvanize action. Only after more decades of patchwork fixes and dilatory discussion was the decision made not to demolish the building – a course favored in some quarters – but to modernize and enlarge the Capitol. A competition was held and a Norfolk architect, John Kevan Peebles, was chosen to design the improvements in 1904. He proposed adding wings to the main block but in such a way, Peebles wrote, so as to "disturb no lines of the present structure." The wings were to be smaller and shorter, their footprints set toward the rear of the original building. Passageways in connecting hyphens would link a new House of Delegates in the east wing and the Senate to the west.

The rebuilding campaign was more expeditious than the original construction, lasting from August 1904 to January 1906. Sadly, it was no less ambitious. Before the wings were added, the original structure was completely gutted. Only the exterior walls were left standing. Selected early wooden elements survive, some of them in the central hall, but almost nothing else in the interior is original. The renovation incorporated new marble floors, a steel super-

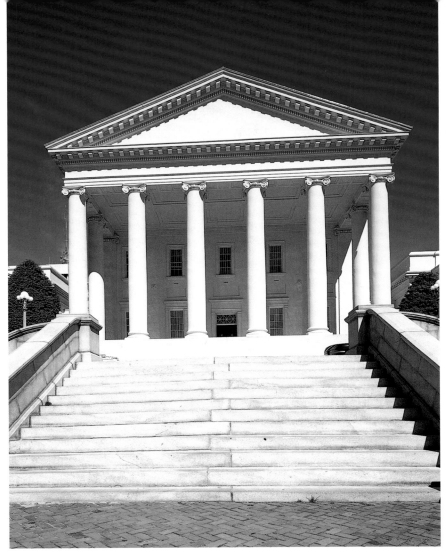

Thomas Jefferson described his Capitol this way: "The capitol is of brick, one hundred and thirty-four feet long, seventy feet wide, and forty-five feet high, exclusive of the basement. Twenty-eight feet of its length is occupied by a portico of the whole breadth of the house, showing six columns in front, and two intercolmniations in flank. It is of a single order, which is Ionic; its columns four feet two inches diameter, and their entablature running around the whole building. The portico is crowned by a pediment, the height of which is two ninths of its span."

structure, elevator, ventilation ducts, and terra cotta and plaster surfaces to fireproof the building. On the exterior, the columns were modified, the shafts reinforced (increasing their diameter), and new bases and capitals fabricated. But there was one Jeffersonian element that had been missing which was finally added, namely the granite steps descending from the front portico to grade.

The Jefferson-Clérisseau collaboration is memorialized by a second, smaller building. This one is nineteen inches wide, thirty-two long, and sixteen inches high.

Precise, scale models were all the rage in France and Italy at the time, and at Jefferson's behest Clérisseau commissioned a Parisian model maker named Jean-Pierre Fouquet to make a model of the Capitol. It was an atypical job for Fouquet, as virtually all of his known works are of idealized antiquities rather than new buildings. But Jefferson regarded the model as a "necessity" and Fouquet was the best man available. As Clérisseau's son-in-law, Jacques-Guillaume Legrand, an architect of note in his own right, later described Fouquet's work, "[T]he best made [models] are due to the very distinguished talents of M. Fouquet, architectural modelmaker, and that he has achieved perfection concerning correct proportions and precision in forms."

At fifteen guineas it was expensive, Jefferson reported, and would add roughly a third to the design cost. But he knew from his abortive experience in portico building at Monticello that Virginia workmen

Jefferson didn't design the White House. There's never been the slightest suggestion that he did. On the other hand, that wasn't because he didn't want the job.

As President Washington's Secretary of State, Jefferson proposed a competition to produce a suitable design for a presidential palace. On March 14, 1792, an announcement drafted by Jefferson was approved for publication by the commissioners of the federal city. It offered a $500 premium for "the most approved plan . . . for a Presidents House." Entries submitted by July 15th were reviewed by President Washington and the three commissioners. Irishman James Hoban was declared the winner and retained as superintendent of construction. The history of what later became known as the White House is a long and densely plotted narrative involving fires, numerous renovations, and much presidential politics, but our protagonist, Thomas Jefferson, Architect, was only an occasional character in the drama at Mr. Hoban's mansion.

A more interesting role of Jefferson's remained secret until early in the twentieth century. Jefferson himself, we now know, had entered the competition anonymously, submitting drawings bearing the initials "A. Z." Somehow his drawings, along with Hoban's and the submissions of three other entrants, found their way into the hands of Benjamin H. Latrobe, surveyor of public buildings between 1803 and 1811. The portfolio containing these drawings was handed down to Latrobe's son, John, who, in turn, presented them to the Maryland Historical Society in 1865. There they gathered dust for some fifty years until a young scholar named Fiske Kimball identified five sheets as unmistakably the work of Jefferson. Until then the "A. Z." drawings had been mistakenly attributed to a Maryland builder named Abram Faws.

Jefferson's rediscovered drawing – and his anonymous competition entry – for the president's house. Courtesy of the Maryland Historical Society.

Jefferson's design has been dismissed by one Palladio scholar as "all too literally stolen" from the Venetian master. That it is an exercise in adaptive Palladianism is undeniable; it's certainly derivative and perhaps ill-conceived (the four grand porticos, one on each side of the square footprint, would have been unwieldy even in a more secure time). Whether it's distinctly inferior to Hoban's design is debatable; Hoban's original renderings were significantly improved by later Latrobe modifications and in its original form, Hoban's design was also derivative, indebted to a plate from James Gibbs' Book of Architecture *(1728) and to Leinster House in Dublin.*

Perhaps a more useful way to consider Jefferson's president's house is in a biographical context. His design is quite evidently the work of a journeyman not yet ready to quit the employ of his master. Jefferson was, after all, an inexperienced designer and builder. He had worked at Monticello for more than a decade, but he had already announced his intention to remodel the home in radical fashion. His only other known work was the Virginia Capitol, which was closely modeled on an existing building, had been designed in tandem with the professionally trained architect Charles Louis Clérisseau, and was built with little first-hand supervision from Jefferson. Even Jefferson's drawings for the president's house betrayed his inexperience, as his draftsmanship looks amateurish next to Hoban's.

It is in the parts rather than the whole that glimpses of Jefferson's design talents lie. Ever desirous of natural light, Jefferson cleverly added skylights to the pyramidal roof. His dome was to be based upon the one he had seen only a few years earlier at the Halle aux Bleds in Paris. He didn't get to build it in Washington, of course, but similar domes were to rise at Monticello and the Rotunda at the University of Virginia. Jefferson sought to create an ennobling architecture for America; knowing what he did about the skills and materials available, he adapted his aspirations to the limitations posed by what was at hand in the nascent capital. In fact, a decade later President Jefferson, recognizing the need for professional architects, established the post of surveyor of public buildings and appointed Latrobe. The thinking he did for the competition may not have amounted to a successful entry, but there were notes and notions in both the design and its practicality that suggest greater things were to come.

Even though Jefferson didn't get the commission, there's a certain poetic justice in that the winning design incorporated a projecting oval room, a feature more than a little reminiscent of Jefferson's beloved Hôtel de Salm, the French house that had been a key inspiration for Monticello II. (The oval room notion may actually have come from Jefferson, since he had written to Washington suggesting that the presidential palace ought to resemble "the celebrated fronts of modern buildings which have already received the approbation of all good judges." He went on to cite the Hôtel de Salm specifically.)

A few years later, Jefferson also got to have significant input at Hoban's manse via another route. When he took office as president in 1801, the president's house was far from finished. In his two terms he was able to exercise considerable influence on its appearance, particularly on the interior, both directly and indirectly thanks to his appointment of Latrobe. Together they agreed upon the curved south portico and added the colonnades that extended from either end of the president's house to connect the executive offices.

were "not very expert in their art." Perhaps he saw the model as good public relations, too, a selling tool that might help dispel lingering doubts about the appropriateness of his plan. What he could hardly have anticipated is that it would prove to be the best surviving record of the design work he did with Clérisseau, since the Clérisseau drawings of the Capitol were lost. They were loaned in 1791 to Pierre-Charles L'Enfant, who at the time was planning the new Capitol City. The tin case containing the architectural renderings was never returned, and its whereabouts remains unknown to this day. That has made the surviving drawings by Jefferson more precious, but they tell us little about the final drawings or the work of the Frenchman. As a result, the plaster model is a key puzzle piece. The model was completed in June 1786; after an unexplained delay, it was shipped off in December, arriving in Richmond well into the building program. No doubt, however, it was a useful reference even if undertaker Dobie didn't feel obligated to copy it slavishly.

The subsequent history of the model has its predictable moments. It's been repaired periodically, its plaster patched. A rear wall was shortly added, probably to stabilize the original front façade, side wall, and roof. The Fouquet model has been on display more or less continuously, spending most of the twentieth century in the Capitol entry hall, having been housed in the Executive Mansion, the governor's Federal Style residence adjacent to the Capitol, for most of the nineteenth century.

While at the Executive Mansion, the model was painted regularly. The result was a thick coating that blurred the architectural details. Recent X-ray images of the model have revealed astonishingly fine detailing beneath. The architraves and cornices were decorated with moldings rendered in exacting detail. The columns, capitals, and garlands on the inset panels between the windows were similarly refined.

The estimated twelve or more layers of paint obscured much of Fouquet's workmanship, but they had their own story to tell. Beneath the extensive *cracquelure* (crackling) of the model's dingy surface lies a veritable palette of colors, including dark green, yellow, buff, black, reddish brown, and several shades of gray. A study correlating paint analysis conducted on the model with historic images of the Capitol revealed both had a series of two-tone color schemes, such as yellow ocher with white in 1830 and dark gray details with pale gray walls circa 1890. Today's all-white building (and model) are consistent with a 1790s whitewashing as well as paint applied after the building was remodeled in the first decade of the twentieth century. In short, as the conservator who directed the recent conservation of the model, F. Carey Howlett, concluded, the model "may bear a more comprehensive history of the paint changes than the heavily altered building itself."

The model is still a model but in subtle ways its role has evolved. Fouquet made it to serve as a reference for the Virginia builders; they, in turn, were engaged in creating a building the likes of which they had never seen, aside from Fouquet's tiny but uncanny miniature. It served its original purpose, but Fouquet's little jewel box now has a richer and more complex significance.

Once the Capitol itself was completed, the model was no longer a reference tool but, by default, it became an artifact. Its caretakers were no longer builders; it became an *objet d'art* on display in the Executive Mansion. The model was to be admired, examined, even studied by visitors, though it was no longer a utilitarian object but a decoration.

Somehow, like the little engine that could, the model kept working. When the Capitol was painted, so was the model. The applications of paint may have obscured much of Fouquet's detail but in the process they added importance, especially after the Capitol itself was skinned and stripped in the 1904-06 remodeling. Almost a hundred years later, its new custodians glimpsed the model's exquisite details using sophisticated imaging technology, and its status was changed once more. After a debate whether to restore the model to original condition, the current caretakers decided the best course would be to make a second model, reproducing as precisely as possible the original appearance of Fouquet's. The model Jefferson sent has been stabilized, yet will remain unrestored, a miniature record of a much used and abused historic building.

All of this has made the model an accidental time capsule, suggestive of the Capitol's evolution, as well as its designers' original intentions (in Clérisseau's case, viewing the plaster building was as close as he ever got to seeing the building itself since he never came to America). Neither Clérisseau nor Jefferson could have predicted how invaluable the model would prove two centuries later when historians attempted to understand better the history of the building itself.

On the other hand, Jefferson fully anticipated that the full-scale building would became a pattern, a model, for the country as a whole.

Although there is no evidence to suggest that Jefferson imagined a dome over the central rotunda in the Capitol, the monumental space has looked as it does since the 1904-1906 remodeling.

Once it dominated its hilltop site like a seven-footer coaching small children, but today the Capitol is hunkered down amid twentieth-century towers in Richmond's dense and modern cityscape. Even though the original scale of the building has been lost, its power to impress endures.

❧

The Virginia Capitol is one of those landmark buildings like the White House, for example, whose historic richness must be appreciated largely from the exterior (in the case of the White House, it's been gutted not once but several times). The Capitol may not be what it once was yet, somehow, even in its radically renovated state, it conveys its message.

The design of the Capitol (and, to a lesser degree, its construction) brought about a personal transformation in Jefferson. As a young man, he had had no option but to teach himself architecture; in mid-life he was quick to open other peoples' eyes to good design. The Virginia Capitol was his first public effort to that end, the University of Virginia his last.

He no doubt learned many important lessons in Richmond that contributed to his maturation as an architect, but surely one of the most important was, *To get what you want, you gotta be there.* He wasn't on site for the construction, and he was never entirely satisfied with the Capitol. Upon first seeing it in 1789, he promptly wrote to his old friend William Short in Paris, confiding that "when the corrections are made . . . it . . . will be an edifice of first rate dignity." Jefferson always had difficulty with leaving off at the close of a job.

His architectural career would follow no logical path, and this important commission has its share of oddities, too. As we've seen, the cornerstone and much of the foundation were laid

before the plans arrived, and installation of the grand main stair was delayed for more than a century after the building's initial construction was completed. But my favorite moment of asynchrony was Jefferson's visit to the building that inspired him.

Despite its fame and beauty, the Maison Carrée in Nîmes is a deceptively simple building. The temple Jefferson saw has remained essentially unchanged for two thousand years. It's rectangular in plan, with a portico of six columns, topped by a gable roof. The portico stands before a windowless box that has pilasters surrounding it. The whole structure is set on a raised basement or pedestal. The architectural order is Corinthian, with olive leaves decorating the capitals.

Of all the visitors it has pleased over the millennia, perhaps none fell harder for the Maison Carrée than Jefferson. He was so enraptured on his visit that he wrote Madame de Tessé, "Here I am, Madam, gazing whole hours at the Maison quarrée, like a lover at his mistress."

What I find most intriguing about that letter to his Parisian friend isn't his passion but the timing. The letter was written at the temple itself as Jefferson joyfully absorbed the great building. That's not the surprising bit – what got me thinking is that he composed the long, architecturally impassioned letter in March of 1787, more than a year *after* dispatching the plans for his Virginia version. Ironically, then, he was inspired by a building he had never seen first-hand to design a building that he didn't get to see for four years. Yet there's nothing out of character in Jefferson poring over books and then envisioning something else altogether, as his political philosophy – so essential to the invention of our nation – demonstrated.

Jefferson's Capitol has long been acknowledged as the first pure temple in American architecture, and from the start his intention was to inspire in others a passion for the classical. The Capitol was his answer to the question he posed to James Madison in a letter written during the months of 1785 that he worked on the Capitol design. "But how is a taste in this beautiful art to be formed in our countrymen," Jefferson asked his good friend, "unless we avail ourselves of every occasion when public buildings are to be erected, of presenting to them models for their study and imitation?" He did exactly that, and others followed, judging from the countless American capitols, court houses, schools, and other civic buildings in classical dress that came after.

For purposes of typology, both Jefferson's Capitol and the Maison Carrée are classified as temples, although the Richmond Capitol memorialized not religious faith but a belief in democratic principles. Jefferson reinvented the Maison Carrée as a temple of reason. The use to which Jefferson put the building had no immediate precedent in America or Europe; the government in the emerging nation was unlike any that came before. The Capitol was the first building designed specifically to accommodate elements of a government with two legislative bodies, a judiciary, and a chief executive. Jefferson's genius was to recognize that the virtues of the temple form could compliment rule by the people. The Founding Fathers sought to establish a government based on such ideals as truth, liberty, and simplicity (in contrast to the bondage of wealth, rank, and overrefinement in England and Europe); the temple form brought an added endowment, that of great dignity. What Jefferson scholar Kimball called the "simple and lucid temple form" may be just a gabled box, but it has an in-your-face portico and stands monumentally tall, commanding its site. It comes with a sense of unity yet grandeur; of strength yet accessibility. To put it simply, to see it is to understand it.

Major Pierre Charles L'Enfant is usually cited as the designer of Washington, D.C. While he was the central player in the early stages, to give him blanket credit is to oversimplify, not least because L'Enfant was summarily dismissed less than three years into the process. A clear case has been made crediting not one man but the triumvirate of President Washington and Secretary of State Jefferson, together with L'Enfant. The three shaped the plans for the city and its two focal buildings, the president's house and the Capitol.

Washington was intimately involved in the decision making and, as his Secretary of State, Jefferson had direct authority over L'Enfant. Always the architectural propagandist, Jefferson saw the new federal city as an opportunity to provide citizens of the new country with a distinguished architectural paradigm. He brought to bear what he had learned in Europe during his five years as Minister to France, sending L'Enfant advice and plans of various European cities. "Whenever it is proposed to prepare plans for the Capitol," Jefferson wrote, "I should prefer the adoption of some one of the models of antiquity which have had the approbation of thousands of years."

He plumped for the Pantheon in Rome as a paradigm for the Capitol; his drafting tools always at the ready, he prepared preliminary sketches. His surviving floor plan incorporates elliptical rooms for a lower level. Since those early studies had no particular impact on the Capitol as built, their significance lies in the fact they anticipate his design some twenty-five years later for the Rotunda at the University of Virginia, a half-scale Pantheon, complete with elliptical basement rooms. Jefferson could be an economical man, and he often recycled his design ideas. (Jefferson also went so far as to enter — anonymously — the design competition for the President's House; for a fuller discussion of his design, see "The President's House," page 76.)

In 1793, Jefferson and Washington personally chose Dr. William Thornton's belated submission as the winner of the design competition for the Capitol. Shortly thereafter Jefferson retired to Monticello for several years but, when he returned as president, he personally involved himself in countless decisions about the Capitol. He found himself arbitrating between its original designer, the amateur Thornton, and Benjamin Latrobe who, as surveyor of public buildings, was charged with managing its construction. In the end, Jefferson got his way, more or less, as both the Capitol and the president's house were far from provincial. Hoban's rendering of a grand eighteenth-century English house and Thornton's monumental Capitol aspired to grandeur. Jefferson succeeded in exercising considerable influence during the prolonged construction of the Capitol, the president's house, and the emerging city.

In considering Thomas Jefferson, Architect, however, neither building is in any sense part of his oeuvre. *Yet Jefferson's supervision of the work in Washington was invaluable experience and in the following decade he would find himself embarking upon another public project, this one the new university in Charlottesville. Though smaller in scale than the federal city, the University of Virginia required a range of expertise in administration and design, as well as managing material acquisition and a large pool of labor. Surely Jefferson was better equipped to face the challenge of building a university on a vacant hilltop having played a key role in the emergence of the city of Washington.*

In a larger sense, too, he succeeded in establishing a new, high standard for the "taste of the new town" — and for the nation as a whole.

Dwellings for Family and Friends

"With Mr. Jefferson I conversed at length on the subject of architecture. Palladio, he said 'was the bible.' You should get it and stick close to it. . . . He is a great advocate of light and air – as you predicted he was for giving you Octagons. . . . In a word, the old Gentleman entered . . . with great zeal into your building scheme and I now regret more than ever that you did not see him."
  – Colonel Isaac Coles writing to
  John Hartwell Cocke, 1816

As one Jefferson scholar observed to me, "He did a lot of scribbling on cocktail napkins." The observation sounds anachronistic – certainly beer nuts, juke boxes, and paper napkins were all invented well after Mr. Jefferson's era. Nevertheless the description is as apropos as an olive in a martini.

The Barboursville ruin, burned on Christmas Day 1884.

85

His friends knew of his enthusiasm for buildings – how could they not, the countless Virginians and others who passed through the portals of Monticello during the fifty-six years he lived there? It was one of the longest-running architectural open houses in American history. People came to visit, found accommodations, enlightening conversation, fine food and wine, plus they got the chance to witness the ever-evolving work at a perpetual construction site.

Jefferson's personal commitment to the power of buildings as an edifying social force was a matter of public record. In his private life, too, his passion for buildings – his own and other people's – was well known. It's no wonder, then, that his Works in Architecture extend beyond his two homes and his two well known public projects, the Capitol and the Academical Village.

Jefferson was always ready to reflect on an interesting architectural challenge, looking for ways to use the past. Never was this more true than in 1793 as he planned his retirement. He had been a lightening rod for political calumnies, some of which even questioned his patriotism. He had had enough, he confided to family and friends, and he eagerly anticipated a permanent withdrawal from public life. He wanted to return to his mountain top, remodel his house, manage his plantations, and watch his grandchildren grow up. It's hardly surprising that over the period of the next several years he came as close as he ever did to taking on architectural clients. To put it another way, during these years away from public service he liberated his left brain in his favorite way by employing his spacial imagination not only at Monticello but also for the benefit of like-minded, historically conscious friends and family.

As an accidental architect, however, Jefferson left only a haphazard record of work done for friends. Some of his correspondence alludes to various designs he did for other people; some drawings in his hand for these houses exist, too. But attributing buildings to him requires a careful and wary eye. His connections to some work, such as the addition at Farmington in Charlottesville and the manse at Barboursville, are beyond dispute. And there are other designs that can be linked to him in various ways, though at times the connection grows tenuous. His advice wasn't always followed; certainly there are missing letters and drawings.

In the twentieth century his architectural output expanded artificially. Particularly in Virginia, there was a Washington-slept-here mentality about fine brick homes of a certain vintage. If Jefferson had designed all the homes that have been linked to him over the years, he wouldn't have had time to be President. It is distinguishing between such claims – which range from the certain to the silly – that make this something of a detective story.

Consider an intriguing case in point, the circa 1765 plantation home called **BRANDON**. It is located midway between Williamsburg and Richmond on the James River. According to oral history, Jefferson was a groomsman at Benjamin Harrison's wedding. For some years, it was believed that an architectural rendering in Jefferson's hand was of Brandon. More recently, a scholarly consensus has emerged that the drawing was an early working sketch for Monticello. Yet there remains the enticing thematic connection between Jefferson and the Harrisons, and the probability that the same eighteenth-century English architectural volume, *Select Architecture* by Robert Morris, was a source for both Jefferson *and* Brandon's designer. In the inbred world that was eighteenth-century Virginia, Jefferson probably had little or nothing to do with planning Brandon although more than likely he and Brandon's designer – whoever he was – were acquainted.

A second house called **FARMINGTON**, located outside of Louisville, Kentucky, begs for another judgement call. It is very tempting to welcome it into the fold since Jefferson, perhaps more than any other American leader of the rev-

A certifiable Jefferson design, this is Farmington, just outside Charlottesville. As was often true of Jefferson designs executed under other people's supervision, the finished building differs a good deal from the original conception. The full entablature on the portico didn't extend around the building but was abruptly abbreviated where it joined the main block. Jefferson also thought the columns were poorly proportioned. There are other discrepancies from his drawings, but the building retains a distinctly Jeffersonian character.

olutionary generation, saw the American west as essential to the country's future. It was he who sought what came to be the Louisiana Purchase and closed the deal – not solely because he feared French ownership of the lands, but because he had a majestic vision in which the United States stretched across the continent. So wouldn't it be convenient if Farmington in Kentucky could be proven to be by Jefferson?

At best, however, the house is a maybe. No documentary evidence survives that connects Thomas Jefferson, Architect, to this project. We do know he was acquainted with the lady of the house, Lucy Gilmer Fry, and that both she and her husband, John Speed, had moved westward from Virginia. The story gets interesting when the plan of the 1815-1816 house is compared to an unlabeled drawing of Jefferson's. That drawing – supposing it indeed was the source for the house — was certainly not used as drawn, since the porticos were shifted and his alcove beds eliminated. Yet the basic arrangement of the house is distinctly reminiscent, since it features four square rooms, one on each corner, with a pair of octagonal parlors in between. The finish of the house is not Jeffersonian in the least (it might better be described as "Kentucky Federal," with delicate mantels, columns, and other details that have a lightness about them in contrast to Jefferson's usual boldness). But the research goes on . . .

In other houses, more Jefferson connections have been identified. Some have family ties, others stylistic similarities. Documentary evidence makes some attributions quite certain, but others, in the language of art history, might be better classified as "in the school of." Jefferson's legacy has a wealth of houses with indirect associations, and they are the subject of Chapter 6 of this book (see page 169). But here in this chapter we'll examine houses, most from the first dozen years after his return from France, when he began to use his designing skills for other people. It was a time when Jefferson — first as secretary of state and, later, as president, was the most powerful architectural authority in the nation. In these cases, though, it was less an exercise of sheer clout than a series of generous gestures to friends and family. In more or less chronological order, then, we'll look at a number of Jefferson — and Jeffersonian — designs.

For many years, **CARRSBOOK** came complete with a tidy little tale of how Jefferson helped his favorite nephew, Peter Carr (1770-1815), build himself a high-style house overlooking his thousand-acre plantation. Unfortunately, the story is a model for how myths can be made using a mix of historical fact and unproven supposition.

The known facts are these. Peter Carr's father died when the lad was three. Since the elder Carr had been both Jefferson's dear friend and his brother-in-law (Peter's father had married Jefferson's sister, Martha), his remains were buried at Monticello. Young Peter and his family then moved to Jefferson's mountaintop, where the future president personally supervised the boy's education, even engaging James Madison to help during Jefferson's years abroad as Minister to France. Jefferson's assistance to his nephew extended to helping the young man both gain entrance to William and Mary and then to read law with Jefferson's old mentor, George Wythe. Carr entered the bar in 1793 and lived at Carrsbrook, a Palladian-inspired five-part manse in Charlottesville. Perhaps he never lived up to the expectations one might have for Jefferson's pet pupil, but he did serve in the Virginia House of Delegates and as Jefferson's private secretary during his presidency. Like his uncle, Carr admired nothing more than book learning and he established a short-lived academy at Carrsbrook, probably to make money. Later he had a role in the conception of the University of Virginia as the recipient of a famous Jefferson letter in which the former president outlined the principles of education.

If the foregoing are the facts, the story hereafter becomes less reliable. Carrsbrook — or "Carrs-brook" or "Carr's-Brook," as the name is variously configured — was long believed to have been built in 1794 on land Peter Carr inherited from his grandmother. That certainly fits conveniently into the narrative, as Carr, just embarking upon a legal career, might well have been ready to settle down, build a house consistent with his prospects, and get married, as indeed he did in 1797. But research has shown that the grandmother in question, Barbara Overton Carr, didn't own the land. Other documentary sources suggest the house might have been built earlier, probably before 1790 and not for Peter but his uncle, Captain Thomas Carr. Certainly, the property came to him later (probably in 1798), but the house is unlikely to have been a collaboration between Peter and his other doting uncle, Thomas Jefferson.

Carrsbook was built before 1790 and for many years was attributed to Thomas Jefferson, Architect. Though a handsome house, the gawky, country-boy feel to its tall assemblage of matchbox forms makes the Jefferson credit unlikely.

At William Madison's home, The Residence, the original Jefferson conception is still discernible, although later remodelings left it with roof lines galore and a zig-zag footprint.

So what about a Jefferson connection? To look at the house closely is to distinguish the likely influence of Jefferson's two favorite architectural volumes, namely Palladio's *Four Books* and Robert Morris's *Select Architecture*. From the time of construction, it was one of Albemarle County's most significant houses (according to tax lists of the time Carrsbrook was valued at $4,000, while the most valuable were Farmington and Monticello at $9,000 and $7,500, respectively). In fact, to look at the house is to be reminded of another probably fictive Jeffersonian attribution, the Finnie house in Williamsburg (see page 24). Both are symmetrical wood-frame houses with some classical detailing. Carrsbrook in particular, with its tall central block trimmed with a heavy modillion block cornice has less of the academic character one would expect of Jefferson's scholarship than of less bookish builders.

So no, a Jefferson attribution won't stick to Carrsbrook. On

Edgemont, in South Garden, Virginia, didn't look like this when it was constructed circa 1794-96. Nor, for that matter, did it look quite the same when it was "rediscovered" in 1936.

the other hand, the inspiration for this house came from somewhere: the five-part Palladian plan was not a common architectural form, and there weren't many people other than Jefferson in central Virginia at that time who aspired to build houses in a classical vein. And Jefferson was the big man on campus even before he invented the campus – Founding Father, former Virginia governor, a truly international figure who knew everybody who was anybody in Charlottesville. What are the chances this house got built without its builder/designer making reference to the Great Man? Close to zero.

Today the house, once at the heart of a plantation bounded by the south fork of the Rivanna River, is screened from its many neighbors by tall trees. What was once open agricultural land is now forested and contains a neat subdivision aptly called Carrsbrook, about equidistant from Charlottesville's airport and its downtown business district. And the house is a handsome survivor of a somewhat Jeffersonian past.

"I have scribbled," Thomas Jefferson wrote in 1793, "on a separate paper some general notes on the plan." He was responding to his old friend James Madison who, on behalf of his youngest brother, William, had asked Jefferson to review some sketches. The younger Madison had briefly read law with Jefferson a decade earlier.

"I have done more," Jefferson's letter continued. "I have endeavored to throw the same area, the same extent of walls, the same number of rooms, & the same sizes, into another form so as to offer a choice to the builder.

When a late nineteenth-century kitchen wing was removed, Edgemont's restorer, Milton Grigg, found evidence of this portico, which was then reconstructed using recycled architectural elements found in the attic.

Indeed, I have varied my plan by showing what it would be with alcove bedrooms to which I am much attached."

Jefferson – perhaps for the first time – found himself designing a house for a friend.

Madison was surprised at the extent of Jefferson's contributions. "[T]hanks for the plans and observations," he wrote back, "[they] far exceeded the trouble I meant to give you." A few weeks later he wrote again, this time with news of William Madison's reactions. "Your plan is much approved and will be adopted by my brother."

While Jefferson's sketches and annotations have been lost, **THE RESIDENCE**, as the house is known, survives as the headmaster's quarters at Woodberry Forest, a private boys'

Again, Grigg used his deductive skills or, perhaps, his imagination when he installed this Palladian screen in Edgemont's entry hall. He identified marks on the floor that suggested its one-time presence, and working from style books, he designed the three-part opening to match the footprint.

preparatory school some thirty miles northeast of Charlottesville. The design wasn't executed as Jefferson drew it, and renovations have changed the place further. Even so, essential elements of the Jefferson formula can be identified (see photo page 90). The house is sited on a hilltop. It is one story tall, the principal living space resting on a raised basement. The roof is hipped, and there's a portico at center front supported by stucco-on-brick Tuscan columns. There are tall windows flanking the front door. The original six-room floor plan resembles other Jefferson works (see especially Edgehill, page 107, and Barboursville, page 112). One can, in short, identify aspects of the house that suggest a Jeffersonian-Palladian parentage, and a cousinly resemblance to Poplar Forest and other Jefferson designs.

But liberties were taken. For example, Jefferson always made careful reference to classical sources, and ancient precedent would have prescribed four rather than two columns and a less steeply pitched roof on the portico. Thanks in part to a Victorian renovation done in the 1880s, the same decade in which the Woodberry Forest School was founded, the house has a strongly vernacular feel. Its higgledy-piggledy additions include matching bay windows on the front, attic dormers, wings at each end, and a small, octagonal turret to the rear.

The Residence, then, is Jefferson in conception but not execution. A skilled local artisan probably built the-home, but did so without the careful supervision of the designer. Jefferson would certainly have preferred masonry to

Though Edgemont is of modest size, it has a surprising dignity, partly attributable to its integration into its rolling landscape. And the house is larger than it appears at first: In the garden elevation pictured here a second, lower floor is visible, having emerged with the change in grade from the front.

wood-frame construction and, had he been at hand, he would have insisted on a more academic adherence to established rules of proportion and detailing. Thus, the significance of The Residence is not that it is prototypical Jefferson; rather, it is likely the first example of his on-again, off-again habit of consulting casually on other people's house designs.

The protagonist was supposed to be the photographer. Frances Benjamin Johnston was a pioneer, a lady in long skirts taking pictures professionally in an era when women didn't *do* that. Her first camera had been a gift from none other than George Eastman. By the time she traveled to Charlottesville in 1936 she had more than four decades of notable work to her credit. She was a documentary photographer and a portraitist whose sitters had included Teddy Roosevelt and Mark Twain. Despite her bona fides, however, the young man she had drafted to be her guide that day, Milton LaTour Grigg, stole the show.

Johnston was surveying Virginia houses on a Carnegie grant. Grigg was a young architect who had been asked by his aunt to accompany her friend Miss Johnston on her rambles. The elderly lady and her bespectacled companion found themselves examining a dilapidated wood-frame house built into a hillside overlooking the south fork of the Hardware River. The structure looked as if it was about to fall down but the sense of discovery must have been palpable. Grigg recognized on first glance what he was looking at: The abandoned, anonymous house before them, he exclaimed, was a lost work of Thomas Jefferson.

Grigg wasn't operating on pure guesswork. Between 1929 and 1933, he had worked in the nascent field of architectural restoration at Colonial Williamsburg. In 1935, he had begun what would be a long relationship with the Thomas Jefferson Memorial Foundation in its restoration of Monticello. He had immersed himself in things Jefferson and, indeed, **EDGEMONT**, as the house they had found was known, spoke to him in Jeffersonian terms. He noted the two Tuscan porticos and a distant resemblance to Jefferson's second home, Poplar Forest, which had also been "rediscovered." Back home, Grigg went to work to prove his hunch and found previously unidentified Jefferson drawings that matched the house.

Grigg didn't stop with the attribution. He persuaded his college roommate to buy the property and, in 1938, work on the 50-by-42 foot house began. He put on two additional porticos, including one on the garden façade where remnants of a foundation were found during excavation. The four porticos made Edgemont a miniature version of one of Jefferson's favorite buildings, Palladio's Villa Rotunda, with its four porches facing the four winds. The design of the last and largest portico was based on the precedent of Poplar Forest with its triple-arch brick arcade on the lower level. Work ceased during Grigg's military service, but recommenced in 1946 with new owners. Grigg interpreted flanking

Belle Grove, in Middletown in Frederick County, certainly speaks for the Germanic origins of its owner with the two-foot-thick local limestone walls. It's a somewhat stolid house – there's a lot of wall space in comparison to window area – and the detailing is a bit crude. But the house probably reflects, in more or less equal measure, Jefferson's plan, local building practices, and the tastes of Isaac and Nelly Hite, who brought to the provinces – this was the frontier – a familiarity with the higher style houses to the east. The west wing was added sometime after 1815.

Golf, anyone? Today the octagonal wing Jefferson designed for Farmington is called the Jefferson Room. It is at the clubhouse of Farmington Country Club near Ivy Creek in Charlottesville.

fieldstone walls extending north and south of the house as evidence of a planned but unexecuted second construction phase. This prompted him to design matching pavilions connected to the house by underground passageways.

Edgemont today is a Palladian statement, a lavish and elegant house, though the mix of original, early-but-adapted, and reproduction elements is a bit confusing. The staircase was transplanted from a house in Charlottesville. Most of the original mantels were in place when the restoration was begun, but the octagonal drawing room had a nineteenth-century mantel that was subsequently replaced with an Adamesque mantel. Some details – egg-and-dart cornice, chair rails, and a ceiling medallion – arrived courtesy of Grigg; the cornice, wainscot, and door and window trim in several other rooms are original.

The current owners have also added to Edgemont's allure, a case in point being the Zuber wallpaper which provides a distinctly French feel to the entry hall. The wallpaper might well have pleased Jefferson whose tastes always inclined to French rather than to English style. Yet for scholars, there are strains of historic disharmony. Some notes are subtle – neither Jefferson nor Palladio, for example, would have been likely to use Tuscan columns and entablature on a house with such rich details (Palladio himself called the Tuscan "a plain and rude order"). In truth, as is often the way with true believers, Grigg's passion for Jefferson had great benefits but also had unforeseen consequences that some find discomfiting in an age leery of conjectural "restoration." Each of the intelligent speculations Grigg made – the Poplar Forest portico, a Palladian screen in the entry hall, the salvaged stairs, the imagined dependencies, the underground passageways, and the rest – are Jeffersonian in their way. Yet they cannot be said to be *by* Jefferson. So in looking at Edgemont today, the first understanding that must be reached is that the place – whatever its merits, and they are many – is as much Grigg as it is Jefferson.

Another issue is whether or not the place is Jefferson at all. Not that Grigg erased all the Jefferson elements – a few, like a dumbwaiter, are gone, but by the standards of his time he was respectful in adding his Jeffersonian touches. No, the question is, *Was Grigg correct in asserting Jefferson designed the original house?* The answer is ambiguous, as there is no documentation establishing beyond doubt that he did. Instead there is an array of evidence to examine and consider.

Jefferson and James Powell Cocke, Edgemont's owner, were contemporaries and neighbors (Monticello is only about ten miles away). Cocke had sold Malvern Hill, a plantation he had inherited in Henrico County, and moved upland, hoping the

climate in the higher elevations of Albemarle County would help him avoid recurrent bouts with malaria. Only one letter to Cocke from Jefferson survives, and it concerns not architecture but the fish that Cocke had sent to stock Jefferson's pond. However, a letter from Jefferson to a third party, dated August 19, 1796, refers to "Mr. Cocke's house" and details the arrangement of certain rooms. Edgemont's plan fits the description perfectly so the assumption is that Jefferson at least visited the house.

According to a Cocke great-grandson, local oral tradition had it that "Edgemont was built for James Powell Cocke by Jefferson's own carpenters." That assertion remains unproven, though there is documentary evidence that Cocke hired a builder, William Bates, to construct ". . . a dwelling house of certain dimensions and rates of work . . . to be completed on or before 1 April 1795." While a good deal is known of numerous builders Jefferson hired at Monticello and, later, at the University of Virginia, Bates is not known to have been among them.

Just as opportunity should never be confused with guilt in a courtroom, coincidence must fall short of proof when it comes to attributing works of art to their (alleged) creators. Yet it is intriguing indeed that when Cocke built his house, probably between 1794 and 1796, Jefferson was on hiatus from public life. After his resignation as Washington's Secretary of State, he remained in residence at Monticello for the next four years. At that time, as well, we know Jefferson was working at the drawings for what would be Monticello II. At the risk of trying on Grigg's conjectural cap, one might hypothesize that Jefferson diverted himself, while drafting plans for his home, by executing a couple of sketches for a friend. As Frank Lloyd Wright liked to say of himself, might Jefferson have let a design drop from his sleeve?

If much of the evidence is circumstantial, the building is surprisingly persuasive. Even if it were stripped of its Grigg clothing, the house has a range of characteristics that Jefferson is generally credited with introducing to Central Virginia (such as the basic configuration with its one-story entrance and two-story garden façade that Jefferson imported from contemporary Parisian designs; the suppressed stairway; the octagonal drawing room; and so on). If it were possible to put Edgemont in a lineup with Edgehill, the house he designed for daughter Martha (see page 107) and The Residence at Woodberry Forest (page 94), one would distinguish a family resemblance between each of the wood-frame, one-story structures, all of which were designed and built in the same decade. Admittedly, no one has found Jefferson's fingerprints, but Edgemont's architectural DNA cannot be lightly dismissed.

There's one last intriguing aspect to the account of Edgemont's reemergence. The great-grandson who reported of "Jefferson's own carpenters," James Powell Cocke Southall, did so in the pages of *Virginia Historical Magazine*. The issue appeared in January of 1935, more than a year before Grigg's and Johnston's visit to Edgemont. In December 1931 a real estate advertisement had been published in the local press that featured a photograph of the house and a description that said it had been designed by Jefferson (the asking price was $20,000, for the house and 392 acres). The question thus arises whether Grigg, the student of Jefferson, could possibly have missed both published references. That seems unlikely.

Bottom line, then, Grigg not only stole the show from Frances Benjamin Johnston, but he also took the lead role from the iconic Thomas Jefferson, thanks to his extensive renovations (as Grigg himself admitted, his work at Edgemont was akin to "putting words in Jefferson's mouth"). We owe Edgemont's survival to Milton LaTour Grigg;

Legend has it that Jefferson ordered the oculus, or "bull's eye" windows, for Monticello but, arriving too late, they were offered to Divers at Farmington. The story is now thought to be apocryphal, although since drawings in Jefferson's hand survive, the Jefferson attribution at Farmington remains beyond dispute.

but it must also be observed that Grigg both reimagined a work of Jefferson's *and*, it appears, even wrote the script for its dramatic rediscovery

In Virginia politics and society, certain names have a way of appearing and reappearing. The same is true in the life and architectural practice of Thomas Jefferson.

The name in the case of **BELLE GROVE** is Madison. This time it's James Madison's older sister, Eleanor ("Nelly"), wife of Major Isaac Hite, Jr., an officer in Washington's army. As with brother William's house, Jefferson — in Madison's words — once again "gave the favor of [his] advice on the Plan."

A mansion house overlooking a large plantation,

The capacious space inside of what is now called the Jefferson Room at Farmington was radically altered in the 1850s when a second floor level was inserted. Today the entire octagon is one large room.

Belle Grove is in the Shenandoah Valley west of the Blue Ridge Mountains. The thumbnail description is familiar: the roof is hipped and the building, though a story-and-a-half tall, is camouflaged as a one-story structure atop a tall English basement (see photo page 98-99). Not only are there similarities to Jefferson's works, but to William Madison's house as well. As one student of both houses remarked, "Woodberry Forest is Belle Grove done in wood."

No one is certain of what role Jefferson played, but there is a letter, written by James Madison to Jefferson, dated October 7, 1794. On his recent wedding trip Madison had spent time in Middletown with the Hites. In writing to Jefferson he said, "This will be handed you by Mr. Bond who is to build a large House for Mr. Hite my brother in law. On my suggestion He is to visit Monticello not only to profit of examples before his eyes, but to ask the favor of your advice on the plan of the house. Mr. Hite particularly wishes it in what relates to the Bow-room and the Portico, as Mr. B. will explain to you. In general, any hints which may occur to you for improving the place will be thankfully accepted. I beg pardon for being the occasion of this trouble to you, but your goodness has always so readily answered such on it, that I have been tempted to make this additional one."

When Mr. Bond, a Quaker mason working in Frederick County in the 1790s, visited Monticello, the place was in an uproar of reconstruction. But the plan for Belle Grove can be seen as a straightforward simplification of Monticello II. Did Jefferson draw

Jefferson's plan for the addition to Farmington. Notice that the elongated octagon was to be divided into two rooms, of unequal size. Courtesy of the Massachusetts Historical Society.

something out for Bond? Perhaps. Did Jefferson show his builder-guest his new plan for Monticello? Probably. Do we know for sure? No.

If the conception of Belle Grove benefitted from Mr. Bond's visit with Jefferson, then the details of Belle Grove, apparently, profited little from Mr. Bond's visit. Researchers believe that he drew upon pattern books, in particular *Pain's British Palladio* (plates from that book have been identified as the design sources for Belle Grove's doorways and mantels and may account for the more vernacular quality of the details). As with The Residence, the local builder paid less attention to classical precedent than Jefferson would have done, yet there are enough common elements to make a Jefferson attribution seem reasonable, among them the suppressed stair and a floor plan very like that of The Residence, Edgemont, and Barboursville.

Inside the house, which was built between 1794 and 1797, there are mantels and fine paneling of the sort that the previous generation would have thought current, including floor to ceiling chimney breasts, wooden wainscot, and strict symmetry of doors, including a fake door in the center parlor. It's a slightly *retardataire* design, but then there's a logic to that, too. Hite was a pioneer in the Shenandoah Valley, one of its largest landholders, and architectural history is full of cases where frontiersmen built not what was trendy but took a more conservative approach.

If Monticello is a feast, then Belle Grove is a simple repast – uncomplicated, traditional, made of good materials and presented with few adornments. It's a practical home for a wealthy landowner who spent his money carefully (the front façade is of cut stone, with corner quoins and ashlar block; the other elevations were built of rubble stone). Given available evidence, this cannot be an ironclad Jefferson attribution, yet there is a strong sense that it's all in the family.

The woman who played the most important role in Jefferson's life wasn't his wife Martha. Nor was it either of the women with whom he had the most controversial relationships, the enslaved Sally Hemings, who almost certainly bore him several children, or Maria Cosway, with whom he had (at the very least) a passionate *affaire de coeur* during his Paris years. He shared a long, measured, and durable friendship with his valued confidant and correspondent, Abigail Adams. Yet none of these women hold pride of place.

His daughter, Martha Jefferson Randolph (1772-1836), proved to be his anchor. She spent more hours in his company and years in his homes than anyone else. She was born (and possibly conceived) in the South Pavilion or "Honeymoon Cottage" at Monticello. At the age of eleven, she and her father traveled to Paris in 1784 where they remained for five years. The year following their return Martha married her cousin, Thomas Mann Randolph, Jr. While the groom's father, Randolph Sr., gave the couple a home, Varina, near Richmond, Jefferson soon prevailed upon the young couple to establish housekeeping closer to him and, in 1793, Jefferson's son-in-law took title to a property named **EDGEHILL**. Jefferson proceeded to design a home for them.

(Note that there would be two Jefferson-related houses on the property called Edgehill, including a larger and later building that became home to his grandson, Thomas Jefferson Randolph, Martha's oldest son and the favored grandson. The second Edgehill, built in 1828, is discussed in the closing chapter of this book since Jefferson did not design it; see page 182.)

The site for Edgehill was a plantation of some 2,000 acres, including land that Thomas Jefferson's father, Peter Jefferson, had purchased and named Shadwell, as well as a much larger parcel of land that came from the Randolph family. But the house was a modest affair, a familiar variation on the plans of Edgemont, Belle Grove, and Woodberry Forest.

Edgehill was never a large house and, by time they took up residence there in 1799, Martha and Thomas Randolph had four children to care for. As more children arrived (remarkably for the time, eleven of the twelve children born to the Randolphs lived to maturity), the house must have been crowded indeed. Fortunately for Martha Jefferson Randolph, Edgehill was more like a home away from home – even during her father's presidency, Martha was usually at Monticello to greet him upon his return from Washington, having herself returned there some days before to get his house in order. It's unsurprising, then, that upon Jefferson's retirement from the presidency in 1809 the Randolphs moved permanently to Monticello where Martha was the lady of the house. She was in residence when Jefferson died and, as his sole surviving child, she found herself at hand when the contents of Monticello and the slaves were dispersed at auction in 1827.

By the time the second home known as Edgehill was constructed in 1828, little was left of the original building. According to a letter written by one Randolph daughter to another, only two rooms remained and "the rest has fallen down." What still stood was moved to the rear of the original site and relocated down a gentle grade. The surviving structure was subsequently adapted as a schoolhouse by Mrs. Thomas Jefferson Randolph in an attempt to lessen the onerous burden of debt inherited from Jefferson. Recent examination of the farm office on the Edgehill property suggests some portion of the structure is original to Martha's Edgehill, but the repeated alterations have been so great the structure is unrecognizable.

Edgehill is a modest one-story house, built on a square footprint with a pyramidal roof. Drawings for it survive and the Jefferson lineage is unmistakable. Courtesy of the Massachusetts Historical Society.

Despite being little more than an architectural remnant, Edgehill is a potent symbol for this period in Jefferson's architectural life. Much of the work from these years shared essential elements, as he proved increasingly proficient at making houses that incorporated academic classicism into forms that suited local conditions. His use of transverse passages across the central block of most of these houses, with entrance halls and parlors on a perpendicular axis, encouraged cooling breezes in the hot Virginia climate. The configuration was unusual in late eighteenth-century Virginia architecture, but we recognize it today as quintessential Jefferson.

Certainly it's no accident that Monticello was close to Edgehill – at a mere four miles' distance, the house was near enough that slaves once carried Jefferson's gravely ill second daughter, Maria, on a litter from Edgehill to Monticello. Jefferson derived pleasure from designing houses, partly because they would be homes for people he loved, his immediate family and a close circle of friends. Just as innumerable contemporary architects began their careers designing homes for their parents, Jefferson began with designs for himself and, in this case, his beloved daughter Martha.

FARMINGTON has a niche of its own among Jefferson's buildings. There he was, in the midst of his great remodeling of Monticello, and along came his friend George Divers. Having built himself a Georgian-style house almost twenty years earlier, Divers was ready for a change, too, so he asked Jefferson if he might update the mansion at his plantation, Farmington. Jefferson,

Over the years, Thomas Jefferson has been credited with designing more than one house for which, we now know, he probably deserves little or no credit. A case in point is Clifton. It got its name — and its Jeffersonian attribution — well after its construction.

To be fair, there is a genuine Jefferson connection. The earliest part of the building was built for Thomas Mann Randolph, Jr., husband of Jefferson's daughter Martha. He and a number of other worthies (including James Barbour of Barboursville, see page 112) attempted to found a commercial town adjacent to the Milton Canal. All that survives of the ill-fated development of North Milton is this house.

Today Clifton bears little resemblance to its original appearance, which probably was a mixed-use office and warehouse. Some remodeling was done in Randolph's life time, as he is known to have taken refuge there while his family traveled with his father-in-law to Poplar Forest. Later, when Jefferson died in 1826, Randolph again retired to North Milton, this time in a fit of pique because Jefferson had not named him executor of his estate. (Randolph was already bankrupt, having been forced to sell Edgehill, see page 107, to satisfy his creditors the previous year).

Despite the ownership and habitation by his son-in-law, there is no evidence in the documents, building fabric, or style of the house to link Clifton to the hand of Thomas Jefferson, Architect (although more than one owner in the past leapt to that conclusion). The viewscape does offer a genuine association in that, from one side of the house, Monticello can be glimpsed on its mountaintop a few miles away.

A series of mid-twentieth-century remodelings gave the original five-room Clifton its Mount-Vernon-style porch and rambling additions. The addition of almost twenty more rooms to the dwelling rendered it quite suitable for its present use as an inn.

The Barboursville ruin remains two stories atop a tall English basement. One has to imagine its original appearance with its hip roof and entrance pediment.

always happy to oblige a friend, got out his pencils and his French weaver's paper with the square grid and sketched both a plan and an elevation of a new east wing for Diver's house (see floor plan page 106).

Construction began in 1802, during Jefferson's first term as president. The portico fronts a tall brick mass built in one of Jefferson's favorite shapes, an elongated octagon. Eight towering triple-sash and nine oculus windows illuminate a single, two-story-tall room inside. If the exterior is imposing – and it is – then the interior is grand indeed. This was Jefferson's light-and-airy manner, and the octagon at Farmington is flooded with sunlight. Several smaller rooms and a passageway of Jefferson's design link the addition to earlier structures on the property.

The house has a long history of change, both before and after Jefferson. When Divers had purchased the plantation just west of Charlottesville in 1785, a log house probably stood on the property; to that Divers had added his brick house. Jefferson's addition came next, and was followed in the early 1850s by a later owner's remodeling. A Greek Revival portico was added to a side elevation, and Jefferson's addition was chopped and channeled into four rooms, two up and two down. Then between 1927 and 1929 the acreage and buildings at Farmington were converted into a country club. Slave quarters, stables, barns, and living areas were adapted to such needs as locker rooms, guest accommodations, and dining areas. Jefferson's elongated octagon became the grand, two-story drawing room it is today.

Despite the changes over time and the builder's failure to follow Jefferson's plan, Farmington's octagonal wing has a cool grandeur that speaks for its designer's ability to adapt his principles and tastes to the needs of a client. The reuse of the structure by the golf club has also meant that the rural setting with its panoramic view of open acreage and the Blue Ridge Mountains beyond resembles what Messieurs Jefferson and Divers saw two centuries ago.

The ground floor of Barboursville once had pairs of rooms at either side, flanking a pair of two-story rooms on the center axis. At the entrance was a hexagonal reception hall with a domed ceiling; behind it an octagonal drawing room looked upon an elaborate formal garden. Jefferson certainly designed a house befitting Governor Barbour's status, although the dome he proposed wasn't built. Courtesy of the Massachusetts Historical Society.

◇

Today the drive from Charlottesville is short, only some twenty miles, but inevitably a visit to **BARBOURSVILLE** is a bittersweet experience. Happily, the place survives, after a fashion. Sadly, it's a burnt-out hulk, a roofless ruin that little more than suggests the original mass of the house as constructed between 1814 and 1822. The brick superstructure is partly obscured by a virtual maze of unruly boxwood, a remnant of an elaborate formal garden. The house, once a paradigm for Jefferson's agrarian ideal, burned in 1884.

      The home was built for James Barbour (1775-1842), a Governor of Virginia and later United States Senator, Secretary of War, and Minister to the Court of St. James. Barbour was a member of Jefferson's circle of powerful Virginians, having grown up on a plantation adjacent to the Madisons' Montpelier.

This is one house that is assuredly part of Jefferson's canon. Detailed written specifications and plans in Jefferson's hand survive, and one reason they do is that Barbour himself wrote to Jefferson on March 29, 1817, expressing his thanks to his friend for his design and returning his drawings. They were hand-delivered by James Bradley, carpenter, the man who built the house. The appearance of the completed house survives only in a photograph and a painting, since all but the brick walls were lost in the Christmas Day conflagration. Several students of Jefferson have suggested the plaster and woodwork inside may have resembled that of Frascati, home of James' brother, Judge Philip Pendleton Barbour (see page 176), but today it's less than a building with no interior floors, blown-out windows, and fireplaces that seem to float in midair. The absence of its roof makes the building the architectural equivalent of a question mark.

Once the nerve center of a traditional Virginia plantation, the Barboursville ruin has an iconic role today as a successful agricultural experiment in an area where Jefferson failed. He had tried repeatedly to establish vineyards in his native Virginia soil (he once described wine as "the only antidote to the bane of whiskey") but he produced not so much as one drinkable bottle. Even so, one can't help but think that the generous-spirited Jefferson would have reveled in touring the hundred-plus acres of carefully tended vineyards that now surround the Barboursville ruin. Barboursville is one of Virginia's largest and most successful vineyards — and if he could visit, Mr. Jefferson would surely have many questions to ask, many notes to make in the notebook he always had at hand. Today the ruin is melancholy, but stands as an important Jefferson work.

If Jefferson's *oeuvre* consisted solely of the work in this chapter — that is, of houses he did for friends and family, then there wouldn't be a strong argument for classifying him as a one of the great American architects. There are individual high points, like the jewel-box Edgemont and the ruin that is Barboursville which, before the fire, most probably was a delight. Taken as a group, however, these houses are perhaps better seen as studies, as off-handed favors akin to holiday-card sketches from the hands of important artists.

To cast them in a theatrical light, these houses can seen as asides, a bit like minor characters in Shakespeare. They gave their creator pleasure; certainly, they amused and even satisfied his friends. But, finally, like Jacques and Polonius and Falstaff, they stand a bit off the main path which, in retrospect, led Jefferson to another set of collaborations which produced a unique set of dwellings in a village of a most novel and wonderful sort. But before he launched his University, he had one more domestic experiment to conduct.

An Escape to Poplar Forest

*"At Poplar Forest he found a pleasant home,
rest, leisure, power to carry on his favorite
pursuits – to think, to study, to read."*
– Ellen Randolph Coolidge

To visit Poplar Forest is to visit an
idea. When construction began at his
Bedford County plantation in 1806,
Jefferson was trapped in Washington
attending to the myriad responsibilities of
an office (the presidency) he hadn't asked
for. We know that during his second
term the job wasn't going terribly well
and that Jefferson daydreamed often of
the day he would retire to Virginia.
Poplar Forest is the bricks-and-mortar
proof of how he translated those musings
into an idealized escape.

Poplar Forest nestled into its verdant setting.

Jefferson liked to reshape the topography of a building site to advantage. He half-buried the dependencies at Monticello; he would terrace The Lawn at the University of Virginia (see page 133); and he contoured the grade at Poplar Forest so that the house upon approach (above) appeared to be one story while the opposite, garden portico stood two stories tall.

Monticello was nearing completion, but President Jefferson realized he had entered the public domain. His mountain-top home had become one of the new nation's intellectual centers, and his life an on-going, forever evolving dialogue on a wide array of subjects. Family and friends by the dozens came to stay at Monticello, and countless strangers climbed the mountain to gawk at the living legend. Jefferson responded to his celebrity by installing a set of blinds, or "Venetian enclosures," around his bedroom suite. On a grander scale, he designed and built Poplar Forest, a home away from home where he could read, think, and maunder without distraction the many matters that interested him.

Jefferson designed Poplar Forest with his own personal uses in mind. Unlike Monticello, which was conceived with Martha Wayles Jefferson and evolved into what historian Merrill Peterson called "a country philosophical hall," the second home in Bedford County was Jefferson's alone. While Monticello was an open-ended exercise in learning architecture, Poplar Forest is a mature work, a culmination of many of Jefferson's ideas about the perfect private house.

The dwelling he built proved most satisfactory. As Jefferson wrote to his old friend William Short in 1821, "I . . . just returned from Poplar Forest, which I have visited four times this year. I have an excellent house there, inferior only to Monticello, am comfortably fixed and attended, have a few good neighbors, and pass my time there in a tranquility and retirement much adapted to my age and indolence." He was hardly indolent, of course, as he was active-

Light is a unifying theme at Poplar Forest. Jefferson continued his experiments with skylights, triple-hung sash, octagonal room shapes, and borrowed light in its clever room arrangement.

ly engaged in designing and supervising the construction of the majestic Academical Village. But for almost twenty years, Poplar Forest provided him the periodic solitude he sought.

Jefferson inherited the 4,819-acre property from his wife's father upon John Wayles' death in 1773. Jefferson inspected his new holdings in Bedford Country that year, but didn't return until he had to. In 1781, he and his family were forced to flee Monticello, warned of the imminent approach of British troops who would have liked nothing better than to take Virginia's governor prisoner. Jefferson took refuge some ninety miles away at Poplar Forest.

He stayed eight weeks, his departure delayed by a fall from his horse. Always one to keep his mind occupied, he wrote much of the only book of his published in his lifetime, *Notes on the State of Virginia*, during his confinement. Perhaps that visit established the notion in his mind that this was a place of respite for him. While that's conjecture, we do know that the existing dwelling on the property wasn't up to his usual standard, as it was an artless overseer's home. His financial records also reveal that in the coming decades Jefferson depended on the income from the property's cash crops, tobacco and wheat. Thus, a combination of factors probably led to his eventual decision to build there.

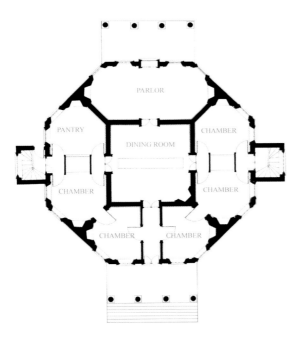

The following labels appear on the floor plan:

PARLOR

PANTRY — CHAMBER

DINING ROOM

CHAMBER — CHAMBER

CHAMBER — CHAMBER

The plan for the main level of Poplar Forest reflects the way the house was to be used. The usual division between private and public spaces was nonexistent, as visitors arriving at the front door traveled through a narrow hall before finding themselves in the cubic dining room at the very core of the house. On the other three sides were doors to two of the bedrooms and the parlor. There were few allowances made for entertaining or even for the flow of servants. Mesick, Cohen, Wilson, Baker, Architects.

In planning Poplar Forest, Jefferson set out to create a pastoral – and Palladian – sanctuary. The first association the word "villa" usually conjures up is of a graceful residence in the bucolic quiet of the countryside and, indeed, the Venetian nobles who commissioned Palladio wanted residences that would enable them to enjoy the cooling breezes in the Veneto and to forget about the odorous canals back in the lagoon. The villa at Poplar Forest was also a place for pleasure, and Jefferson usually brought a pair of beloved granddaughters with him (as one of them, Ellen Randolph Coolidge, later put it, they were there "to make his tea, preside over his dinner table, accompany him in his walks, in his occasional drives, and be with him at the time he most enjoyed society, from tea till bed time").

Just as Jefferson relied upon his Bedford County farms to pay his bills, Palladio's clients had looked to their agricultural holdings on *terra firma* to provide income. The Pisani, the Barbaro brothers, and other Palladio clients wanted country homes that were both mansions *and* farm houses. So did Jefferson. If his days at Poplar Forest were a pleasurable escape from the hurly-burly of Monticello, it wasn't accidental that his visits often coincided with planting and harvest. The villa, both to Palladio and Jefferson, represented a pragmatic mix of work and relaxation, of business and pleasure.

As with most good designs, Poplar Forest's wasn't divined in an instant. Decades earlier, in the 1770's, Jefferson had traced an octagonal plan from *A Book of Architecture* (1728) by James Gibbs. With a rotunda room at the center and two flanking pavilions, it's a recognizable precedent for Poplar Forest, though its intended use was as a garden temple. A decade later he developed plans for a governor's house in Richmond, this time with a true, cylindrical rotunda at its core. Another decade after that, he worked up a plan for the president's house with a similar *schema* (see page 76). But not until Poplar Forest were any of his rotunda house plans realized.

The house at Poplar Forest has the purity of a geometry lesson. Jefferson had been fascinated with octagons since the 1760s, studying designs not only by Gibbs but by other English architectural book authors, including William Kent and Robert Morris. He had seen octagons in Paris and incorporated half-octagonal room ends at Monticello. He liked that an octagonal shape meant that the windows faced not four directions, but eight, increasing interior light and ventilation.

Poplar Forest in its Greek Revival guise, prior to the 1990s restoration. The Corporation for Jefferson's Poplar Forest.

Jefferson didn't build a rotunda, though he did describe the house as being "an octagon 50 f. in *diameter*" (italics added). Instead he chose to insert a perfect cube into his octagon. It's the dining room, at the center of the house, twenty-feet wide, deep, and tall, with an immense skylight (it's sixteen-feet long). Jefferson got so carried away with his abstract musings that he failed to provide stairs from the lower level to main floor, requiring a change during construction. As the building evolved, with porticoes, stairs, and more doorways added, the sharp lines of the ideal softened, and a more practical house emerged.

That isn't to say the design wasn't successful, just unprecedented for a genteel, high-style Virginia home of the time. The bright and generous dining room was a delightful surprise after the dark and narrow entry passage. The parlor

Note the front portico columns are a buff color. Poplar Forest's restoration team has been at the forefront in the "back to the lime" movement in which the lime putty has been made by authentic means, producing mortar, plaster, and lime washes consistent with the original materials. Jefferson never intended the columns to be white – that's a later, Greek Revival affectation – but a textured, stone color.

beyond looks south over the formal gardens – it's a room whose triple-sash give it the air of an orangery.

Jefferson understood that to avoid impossibly complicated rooms of short, oddly-angled walls, the rooms had to be large, and the six-room main floor feels spacious. It's an efficient design, too, with fifteen fireplaces but only four chimneys. Unfortunately, one of them, its flue steeply corbeled from the dining room, was probably the cause of a fire in 1845. Flames consumed the house, reducing it to a roofless ruin. The owner at the time, Edward Hutter, in whose family Poplar Forest would remain for a century, rebuilt the house in the following year, but he paid little heed to Jefferson's original design. He didn't need a retreat; he was engaged in the day-to-day management of a farm. He rebuilt the house in the then-current Greek Revival style, adding a third level with bedrooms and storage over the dining room (abbreviating by eight feet its twenty-foot ceiling). The dining room itself was moved downstairs where a mix of service rooms had been part of Jefferson's original design. Though an appealing amalgam on its own terms, the Hutter-era remodeling obscured one of Jefferson's greatest works for more than a century and a half.

The events of 1845-46 are almost irrelevant to the Poplar Forest story today, as great pains have been taken to erase their effects. Yet the fire was a key turning point in the life of the house, preceded by the story of its construction and followed very much later by its restoration.

Poplar Forest's is not a typical preservation tale in which a fine house is finally given the tender attentions it deserves. Despite the voluminous writings on Jefferson, the house remained until very recently a largely forgotten chapter of his life, with Jefferson scholars as late as the 1950s reporting that "the building is no longer in existence." The house is now open to the public and the astonishing reincarnation is well underway. A disfigured remnant has, phoenix-like, assumed much of its original form. But let's go back in time first, and consider its initial construction.

In the fall of 1805, Jefferson dispatched Hugh Chisolm to make bricks for his new house. Although a veteran Monticello carpenter and brick mason, Chisolm wrote to his employer the following spring requesting help in laying out the foundation (no doubt, consistent with the practice of the day, the drawings were far from complete). So in the summer of 1806 Jefferson traveled to the building site, a trip that proved significant. It led to a September 7th letter in which Jefferson, writing to Chisolm, ordered that two porticos be added, along with "two stairways necessary for communication between the upper and lower floors." Perhaps today we'd call it a change order, but Jefferson's instructions amounted to a virtual reinvention of the house, transforming both its exterior appearance and the interrelationship of the interior spaces. The move was also classic Jefferson — he was never bashful about second-guessing himself and rethinking his plans during construction.

The balusters on the roof parapet are of Honduran mahogany turned in three ever-so-slightly different profiles. The work is new but without tell-tale uniformity.

At Poplar Forest, Jefferson was an absentee builder who visited the site only twice during the first four years of construction. That his day job prevented him from closer supervision proved to be fortuitous for today's restorers. His remoteness from construction meant, on the one hand, that not everything was executed to his high standard (after his second visit, in the autumn of 1807, he wrote to Chisolm to complain of sloppy brickwork, and asked him to come to Monticello "where I wish some work done under my own eye"). A happier result of his absence was that Jefferson, always a copious letter writer, had to resort to pen and paper to communicate his wishes. Some 1,500 letters to and from craftsmen and suppliers have survived, providing an invaluable source in the restoration process.

Without this trove of documents we would know little of construction and, further, the restoration taking place today might not have been possible. Yet other sources of information have offered key insight into Jefferson's vision. A high-tech study of the house conducted by conservators used chemical and even nuclear analysis to produce an array of new understandings about the nature and date of various layers of paint, plaster, and mortar. With exceeding care, the house was stripped and scraped back to its original masonry in a process akin to archaeology. This close physical examination revealed the placement of original and later elements such as chair rails and cornice. Thus, the house itself yielded countless clues about its original, Jeffersonian appearance.

A third source of data has been Monticello, since documentary evidence linked a variety of Jefferson's most trusted craftsmen to both houses. Among them were James Dinsmore, who simultaneously made doors and windows for Poplar Forest and Monticello in his shop on Jefferson's mountaintop in Charlottesville; carpenter John Perry, who installed some of those doors and windows at Poplar Forest, having already framed both Poplar Forest and Monticello (later he would frame other structures at the University of Virginia); painter Richard Barry, who glazed sash and may also have grained doors for Poplar Forest; John Gorman, an Irish quarryman and stonemason who laid the hearths in Poplar Forest before going on to the University where he executed stone capitals, plinths, sills, and wall copings for the

When visitors arrived in Jefferson's time, the face of the house was largely obscured by a wall of poplar trees that gave the house the appearance of having been placed amid a forest. Some of those ancient trees survive today.

The only original wood fabric at Poplar Forest thanks to the 1845 fire that gutted the house is in the matching privys.

Rotunda and the pavilions; and the enslaved John Hemings, Jefferson's most skilled joiner, who executed the classical trim on the interior as well as the roof work, including the decorative railing.

The restorers have found themselves triangulating the documentary findings, physical evidence, and stylistic comparisons in making countless restoration decisions. All of this was essential because, though the brick walls of the house survived the 1845 fire, essentially no details did. The reconstruction the following year made the restorers' job doubly difficult, because extensive changes were made to window and door openings, fireplaces, room configurations, and the shape and pitch of the roof. The alcove beds were not rebuilt, new partition walls and floors were added, and room usages changed. Significant alterations were made in the 1940s, too, when five bathrooms, electric wiring, and other modern conveniences were added.

Looking back through time, the researchers concluded that much of the original interior of the house was completed between 1809 and 1814, though Jefferson was certainly in occasional residence by 1809. The 100-foot long service wing was added in 1814 (Hugh Chisolm was, once again, in charge). Exterior trim was applied in the following year, and interior trim was added piecemeal over the next decade. In an on-again, off-again building programme, the construction required seventeen years (as late as 1822, Jefferson ordered plaster ornaments to complete the friezes in the dining room and parlor). About the time he produced a finished house, however, the aging owner no longer felt able to take the arduous journey to his second home, and gifted the property to his newlywed grandson, Frances Eppes, the only child of daughter Mary (Maria) Jefferson Eppes to survive into adulthood. Eppes moved into Poplar Forest in 1823 and, three years later at Jefferson's death, he was formally granted the house in his grandfather's will. Two years later, however, it was sold out of the family. The house remained in private hands until 1984, when it became the property of a non-profit organization, the Corporation for Jefferson's Poplar Forest, which had been founded the previous year to preserve the property.

The south-facing parlor features four immense windows (two pictured here) and a large double door, welcoming light from a southern radius of nearly 180 degrees.

Jefferson's joy in geometry is evident in his landscape, too. He sited the house on a small rise, and the approach is a long drive, through the open fields and woodlands of the plantation. The immediate landscape around the house is enclosed by a circular roadway, but the access road penetrates the circle like a vector, terminating at a smaller circle, a carriage turnaround immediately before the front door.

The mathematical precision of Jefferson's plan is most apparent when seen from above. The fifty-foot octagonal house rests at the center of the larger circle and, together with its attendant structures, it bisects that circle. Radiating out on each side on an east-west axis were symmetrical rows of trees of that extended to two matching earthen mounds 100 feet to each side. Beyond the conical earthworks octagonal privies survive. The whole assemblage constitutes a uniquely Jeffersonian interpretation of a Palladian plan, with the house at the center as the main block, the trees as connective hyphens, the hillocks standing in for Palladian pavilions, and the outhouses adding symmetrical emphasis. It's an idealized set of figures — including circles, cones, and octagons — all of which extend out from the perfect cube that was the dining room at its very center.

When Jefferson stepped onto the south portico overlooking the garden, he admired a landscape very much of his creation. Due south was a formal parterre, a sunken garden some 200 feet long and ninety or more feet wide. The drop in grade was the result of an excavation (the fill had been used to form the mounds), but it also allowed the lower floor of the house natural light and easy access from ground level. What appeared to be a one-story structure on the entrance façade was, in fact, two stories tall, the house's designer having carefully integrated the house into its landscape.

Upon first seeing another great neo-Palladian house, one wit of the day remarked, "House! Do you call it a house?? Why! It is too little to live in, and too large to hang on one's watch." In fact, Chiswick, built on the outskirts of 1720s London, is hardly small, with a footprint seventy-feet square. But there are some intriguing similarities to – and differences from – Poplar Forest that make these eccentric but pendant-perfect buildings a provocative pairing.

Both were variations on Palladio's Villa Rotonda, but the purposes for which each was built distinguish Chiswick from Poplar Forest. The wealthy Richard Boyle, Lord Burlington, envisioned Chiswick as a showplace, an oversized display cabinet for his *objets*; in contrast, Jefferson's house was an enlarged *cabinet*, in the French sense of a gentleman's private quarters. In their own times and countries, both men cast themselves as publicists for Palladio, though each rummaged freely through the classical past in search of other ideas and details. These men worked largely alone in designing Chiswick and Poplar Forest, though both sought the authority of earlier designers, with Jefferson looking to the books in his library for source material while Burlington the connoisseur studied the original architectural drawings he had collected, which included many by Palladio and Inigo Jones, who a century before had almost single-handedly introduced Renaissance architecture to England. Both men associated with key architectural figures of their day. Jefferson was an *éminence grise* early in the careers of Robert Mills and Charles Bulfinch, and appointed Benjamin Latrobe as surveyor of the nation's public buildings (the latter would also make important contributions at Jefferson's university project). For his part, Burlington counted among his confidants Colen Campbell, William Kent, and Henry Flitcroft.

Chiswick is a much grander building than Jefferson's second home. The stonework is of a quality unheard of in America in Jefferson's day. The scale is larger, the interiors more ornate. Chiswick's gardens are so filled with elaborate temples and follies that Jefferson's conical mounds and octagonal necessaries seem so modest as to be almost bathetic in comparison.

Yet, at least to my eye, those privies are emblematic of the place. Lord Burlington built his house to show off; Jefferson built Poplar Forest because he was weary of being on show. The program at Chiswick isn't so far from Palladio's commission for La Rotonda — both are *villa suburbana* rather than the nerve centers of working farms. But Poplar Forest was never a house fit for an Old World aristocrat. While Monticello is instantly recognizable as a presidential mansion, Poplar Forest can be seen as a house for Citizen Jefferson, complete with the privies that were, unashamedly, incorporated into his landscape plan.

The significance of Poplar Forest stems from its association with Jefferson. Absent the Sage of Monticello from this out-of-the-way, one-time ruin and the place would never have risen from its fall to footnote status. Having offered that disclaimer, however, one can move on to consider it within the context of Jefferson's works and its time and place.

No inventory survives from Jefferson's habitation, but other evidence suggests that the furnishings at Poplar Forest had little of the grandeur of Monticello's. This was a simpler place, as granddaughter Ellen Randolph Coolidge recalled in 1856. "It was furnished in the simplest manner," she wrote to one of Jefferson's early biographers, "but had a tasty air." The rooms were outfitted with Windsor chairs("stick chairs" Jefferson called them), a three-part dining table, several Pembroke (tea) tables, mirrors Jefferson had brought back from France, and built-in alcove beds. This was the largest room in the house, the cube-shaped dining room.

In conception, Poplar Forest had an intellectual courage about it. Jefferson wasn't building in a Virginia idiom (he never did) nor was he simply mimicking classical or Renaissance sources. In the same way he developed his pitch for independence, he began the planning of Poplar Forest in the realm of ideas. On the *tabula rasa* of his Bedford County plantation he envisioned an exercise in pure geometry, a perfect octagon. In execution, the clarity of his vision quickly became clouded by practical needs (the addition of the stair towers and the porticoes), though even then the house retained its symmetry and balance. Then came the east wing, like the outrigger on a canoe, which stabilized the household, making it a more practical place for Jefferson, his family, and servants to reside for sustained periods.

Is it a perfect building? No, of course not (there's no such thing in the real world much less in the world according to Jefferson). The trusted Chisolm built the columns incorrectly, so to this day they fall short of the ideal proportions Jefferson specified. Even if some architects refuse to accept it, every builder understands compromise (Jefferson more than most given his penchant for experiment, in this case with roofing materials and skylights). That meant that his roofs almost always leaked. Francis Eppes' last letter to his grandfather, composed at Poplar Forest only twelve days before the old man died, reported that the roof leaked "not in one but a hundred places."

A visit to Poplar Forest today is not a typical historic house experience. At Monticello, one can imagine that Mr. Jefferson was interrupted moments earlier and left off writing a letter on his polygraph machine to greet an unexpected visitor. At Poplar Forest, such illusions are unlikely. A prolonged restoration campaign is well-advanced but the finished product is still years away. You will see no period room tableaus; no film crews are booking the place to shoot scenes for costume dramas. There are bare masonry walls, a minimum of furniture, and a thousand details yet to be restored.

Yet, in a very real if not literal sense, the place resembles what it would have been like to be a guest of Thomas Jefferson himself in the first years of his habitation. After all, his houses were perennial work sites, and that's exactly what his Bedford County home is today. The restorers are attempting where possible to follow Jefferson's original building sequence, working to finish the building by adding floor surfaces, the alcove beds, and plaster in just the order he did.

Visiting Poplar Forest is its own special reward. Unlike Monticello, this isn't a house with a certified place in America's architectural memory. It was lost and forgotten, which makes its reappearance more remarkable. Today at Poplar Forest the visitor can gain a privileged glimpse of the gears turning as Mr. Jefferson cogitated upon his profoundly personal take on his second home, a country house escape.

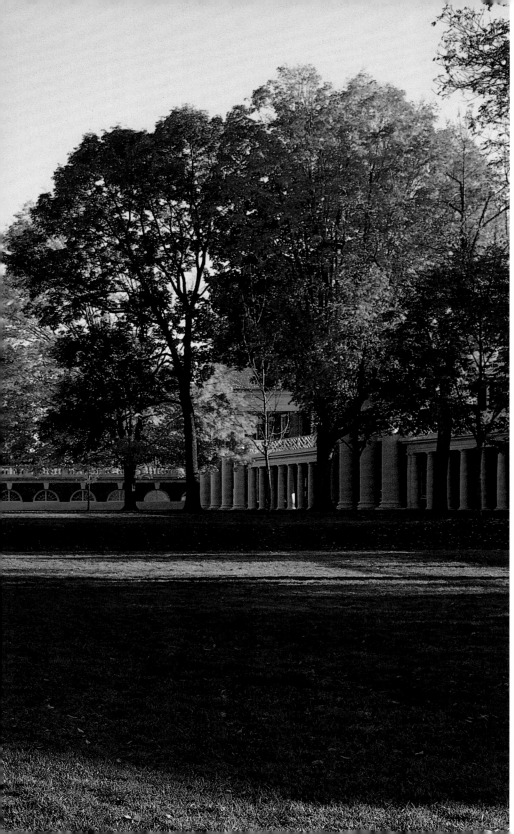

The Academical Village

*"Architecture is the art of organizing
a mob of craftsmen."*
– Geoffrey Scott,
The Architecture of Humanism, 1914

Architecture was not Jefferson's
greatest love . . . learning was. He
devoted his life to acquiring knowledge
about history and "natural philosophy"
(by which he meant, in the terminolo-
gy of his time, the sciences). His studies
led him to master foreign tongues (he
spoke five languages and read seven).
He was a student of agriculture, nature,
technology, and craft. He was devoted
to the arts, including, of course, architecture. All of which put the last great

*The Rotunda overlooking The Lawn at the
University of Virginia in Charlottesville.*

The view from the Rotunda terrace, looking toward The West Range and (right to left) Pavilions I, II, and III.

accomplishment of his life, the establishment of the University of Virginia, at the core of both his architectural work and his life.

His dream of a state-run university has endured. Today the University of Virginia is a top-ranked research institution with an enrollment approaching 20,000 students. But this chapter concerns the original cell of what has become a much larger organism, just as Jefferson anticipated it would. The Jeffersonian precinct draws half a million visitors annually and has been universally recognized as one of the chief accomplishments of American architecture. To visit is to understand why. A walk through the "Academical Village," as Jefferson nicknamed the place, is to experience a museum, cloister, village, college, and a daydream all rolled into one.

The visitor approaches from Charlottesville which, in Jefferson's time, was a small village. Once isolated from the little town, the University is now very much a part of a city that has outgrown its infrastructure. The streets are burdened with traffic. Its boundaries have blurred as new commercial construction lines the main arteries. The surrounding countryside has been annexed by suburban development, and the University itself has become a dense, 1000-acre matrix. But the twenty-eight acres of the Academical Village remain an oasis.

More than forty years before his university welcomed its first student, Jefferson began promoting education reform. In 1779 he drafted a Bill for the More General Diffusion of Knowledge for the Virginia House of

The character of a place is often best judged not by its most dramatic space but by its modest ones, such as its aisles and stairwells. By that standard, the quality of the Academical Village is high indeed, with dramatic walkways like this one, a simple colonnade lined by Pavilions and Dormitories on the right and columns on the left.

Delegates. The legislation was ambitious, calling for the establishment of publicly funded elementary schools, district colleges, and a university (in today's terms, that translates as elementary, secondary, and collegiate education). Primary schools would be built in individual districts or "hundreds" to instruct "all the free children, male and female" in reading, writing, and arithmetic. As students advanced, the system would become selective, with the goal of identifying the best students "without regard to wealth, birth or other accidental condition or circumstance." The complex and considered piece of legislation incorporated specifics as to curriculum, facilities, and staffing.

Although the 1779 bill was tabled, the underlying philosophy was visionary and, in the fullness of time, became received wisdom. Two goals were paramount: first, general education, since Jefferson believed that an educated public was essential to the success of democracy (as he wrote in 1786 to his friend and former teacher, George Wythe, "No other sure foundation can be devised for the preservation of freedom"). The second central principle was equally progressive: as he later wrote to his nephew, Peter Carr (the squire of Carrsbrook; see page 88), the best minds needed to be exposed to "every branch of science, deemed useful at this day, [which] should be taught in its highest degree." In short, he believed – unlike so many of his contemporaries – that everyone should be given the opportunity to learn the basics and the brightest should be exposed to the most advanced thinking of the day (though the enslaved were unacknowledged exceptions).

In 1796, a stripped-down successor to Jefferson's bill, the Act to Establish Public Schools, was enacted. Inadequate funding meant full implementation was impossible, but the attempt was to achieve Jefferson's first aim, that of general education. Jefferson himself continued to consider ways that his second goal might be reached, and regularly regaled visitors to Monticello with his evolving schemes. To Joseph Priestly in 1800, he wrote, "We wish to establish . . . for the State, an University on a plan so broad and liberal and *modern*, as to be worth patronizing with the public support."

Correspondence from 1804 reveals that his continued cogitations on the subject had produced some new thinking about the physical plant for his proposed university. Unlike the school he had attended, William and Mary, where the College had consisted of one large building, he had begun thinking that "a plain small house for the school & lodging of each professor is best. . . . In fact an University should not be an house but a village." Among the advantages he saw were reduced risks of catastrophic fire and transmission of disease. Years would pass before the legislature would act, but Jefferson's notion of a collegiate village was taking shape in his mind. In an 1810 letter to a trustee at East Tennessee College, Jefferson again decried "one large and expensive building," and recommended instead an open square surrounded by "lodges" (for the professors) and "barracks" (for the students), and described the whole as "an academical village."

Back in Virginia, the year 1814 proved to be a turning point. That spring the retired president was appointed a trustee of the Albemarle Academy. At his first meeting he helped engineer the appointment of Peter Carr as board president. The Academy existed only on paper, despite having been chartered years earlier, but Jefferson set to work to effect a conversion of the original state-authorized plan for a secondary school into his long-imagined university. There would be another delay occasioned by the illness and death of Peter Carr in 1815, but in February 1816 a bill was finally passed that established Central College, as well as a Board of Visitors empowered to solicit subscriptions. It was a powerhouse board – the Visitors included James Monroe, James Madison, and John Hartwell Cocke (master of Bremo, see page 172), as well as Jefferson. Just as important, with

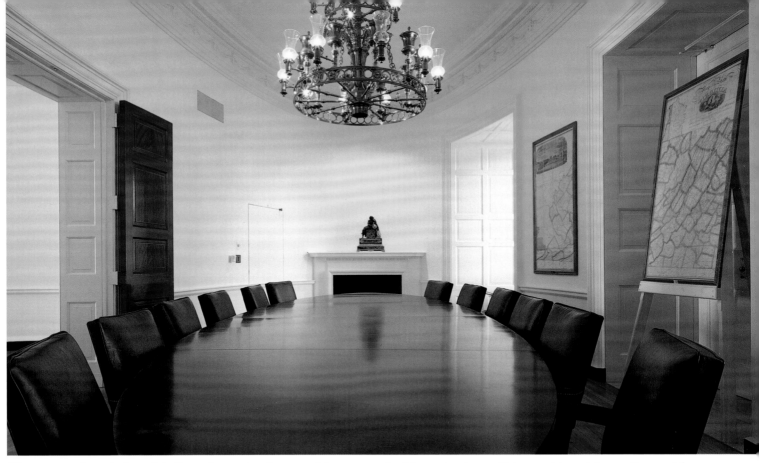

The rooms on the main floor of the Rotunda serve largely ceremonial purposes today. The west oval room (facing page) is used for receptions, and features a Thomas Sully portrait over the mantel. The north oval room (above) is used for meetings and examinations.

the sanction of the Commonwealth of Virginia Jefferson could retire to his drawing board and begin rendering in architectural terms a vessel for his long-simmering idea.

He began with a village square. More a rectangle, really, but with the advantage of historical hindsight, his choice of a geometric figure seems almost inevitable. The enlightened Mr. Jefferson saw in pure shapes a spiritual beauty: the circle, the square, the cube, the sphere, and the octagon spoke to him.

They always had. In Jefferson's surviving drawings is an intriguing antecedent to the site plan he drew in 1814. In 1771 or 1772, the youthful Jefferson prepared a design for the completion of the College of William and Mary at the invitation of the royal Governor of Virginia. He incorporated the existing Wren building that he knew so well into an enclosed quadrangle in the European academic tradition. His approach, which was consistent with the original 1695 plan, won Lord Dunmore's approval, although the rumblings of revolution brought work to a halt before the foundations could be completed. That plan also echoes . . . guess who? Perhaps you've already anticipated the reverberation, but Jefferson predictably hit a couple of Palladian notes that he borrowed from the second of *The Four Books*.

The 1814 plan was a rectangle with a difference. The conventional ivory-tower approach was to regard a college as akin to a monastery, a cloistered place for learning. Jefferson's was a variation on that theme. His incorporated nine dwellings for professors, three on each of three sides, linked by a string of student dormitories, all looking into an open green some 250 yards across. From the center of the grounds, the viewer would see a uniform line of square posts that supported a covered porch or walkway connecting the buildings. Another distinguishing characteristic of his design was the absence of a fourth side. That end was open to the horizon, just as Jefferson wanted the minds of the students and professors to be free and open to new ideas and possibilities. While many of the particulars of this plan were revised in the years to come, the dual sense of enclosure and openness would remain.

In April of 1817, Jefferson and his fellow Visitors selected the site. Once part of a plantation known as Monroe Hill (named for its one-time owner, James Monroe), the acreage was purchased from Jefferson's old retainer, John M. Perry. Perry negotiated into the sales contract for the Monroe Hill property a provision assuring

Construction on Pavilion VII (left) was begun in 1817, Pavilion V (center) the following year. The first was a Jefferson-Thornton collaboration, the second the work of Jefferson, with assists from Latrobe and Palladio.

that he would be among the carpenters and brick masons employed on the project. Perry was just the first of the Monticello workmen that Jefferson would hire to build his university. Within days he wrote to James Dinsmore and John Neilson inviting them to participate in erecting "the great state university." All three would contribute significantly to the character and quality of the finished product.

Jefferson, a trained surveyor, staked out the buildings on July 18th. He had adapted his earlier plan, moving the professors' dwellings (he called them "Pavilions,") into two, north-south rows that faced one another across a two hundred-foot wide green ("The Lawn"). The south end was to remain open, while the north would feature "some principal building." The as-yet unspecified building (it proved to be "The Rotunda" to house the library) would be at the acme of Monroe Hill.

Jefferson had a thing about little mountains, and the property's elevated location a mile west of the town of Charlottesville was among its virtues. But Jefferson's plan called for a site with the topology of a billiard table, and

Monroe Hill was no mesa. It sloped away from its peak, so Jefferson adapted his plan further. He incorporated a trio of terraces into the plan to step down the gentle slope from the site of the "principal building" at the north end of The Lawn. In ways that even Jefferson surely did not anticipate, the irregularity of the site would make the completed village all the more compelling.

The Academical Village was certainly Jefferson's brainchild. He even specified that the epitaph on his gravestone identify him as "Father of the University of Virginia." But other people helped in the birthing. Some of them were tradesmen like Neilson, Dinsmore, and Perry, but at least two others were architects of note. Extensive documentary evidence of the planning and building process survives, but enough is missing that assigning credit for precisely what Jefferson's advisors did and didn't do isn't always easy.

We do know for certain that in May of 1815 Jefferson watched eleven wagons depart Monticello, all weighed down with what he called his "great library" (he accumulated three book collections in his lifetime and this was by far the largest, consisting of 6,487 volumes). He needed the money from the sale, and three quarters of the proceeds went directly to his creditors. The nation needed the books, British troops having burned the Capitol the previous year. Jefferson's great library became the nucleus of the reborn Library of Congress.

Among the carefully catalogued books in their pine cases were forty-nine works devoted to architec-

Jefferson gave the craftsman who were to build Pavilion V these drawings, a Palladio-style rendering of elevation and floor plans together on the same sheet. He also provided detailed specifications for the order to be used, in this case Ionic, from Palladio. The giant columns were the inspiration of Benjamin Latrobe. Thomas Jefferson Papers, The Albert and Shirley Small Special Collections Library, University of Virginia Library.

Although Jefferson originally conceived of the hotels as dining halls, Hotel B in the East Range never served that purpose. Today it houses administration offices, but once was home to the man who managed the construction process, Arthur S. Brockenbrough, and later was a fencing academy.

ture, which constituted one of the finest collections of architectural books in America at the time. Their arrival in Washington would prove a great boon to future users, but their relocation obviously meant that Jefferson no longer had the books at hand. As one for whom books were as essential as planes to a cabinetmaker, Jefferson was handicapped without his trusted sources to peruse. He had immediately begun ordering replacement books, but he also asked for help as he worked at the plans for Central College.

In May of 1817, he wrote to Dr. William Thornton, the winner of the Capitol design competition. Jefferson's letter contained both a description and a rough sketch of the plan for nine professors' dwellings around a common. The Pavilions, he explained, were to be "models of taste and good architecture, & of a variety of appearance, no two alike, so as to serve as specimens for the Architectural lectures." He then solicited Thornton's help: "Will you set your imagination to work & sketch some designs for us . . .?" Thornton's copious reply included a large dose of his own educational philosophy and a sheet of drawings featuring two front elevations, each of a Pavilion with a section of the covered walkway to one side. The first, wrote Thornton, was "a Pavilion for the Centre, with Corinthian Columns, & a pediment." The other was simpler, with a flat roof and Doric columns. He added columns to the walkway and arcades beneath the pavilions.

The first structure to be built, Pavilion VII, appears to have a been a composite of Jefferson's ideas and Thornton's sketch of a front elevation. The building has elements of Thornton's façade, featuring five arches supporting six Corinthian columns, with a Jeffersonian half-round lunette window in the pediment. Jefferson's encompassing walkways are there, too, but as Thornton had recommended, they would be lined with columns. This was a change from the square posts Jefferson originally proposed.

Jefferson appears not have to have been satisfied with Thornton's sketches. Just one day after he received them, he dispatched a letter to another old colleague, Benjamin Henry Latrobe. His request for help of June 12, 1817, also got a generous response. "I found so much pleasure in studying the plan of your College," wrote Latrobe, "that the drawings have grown into a larger bulk than can be conveniently sent by the Mail." It wasn't until August that Jefferson received Latrobe's first rough sketch, but it was worth waiting for. In it Latrobe had drawn the Pavilions with two-story columns (unlike Thornton's elevation sketches of stacked façades consisting of one-story columns on the upper floor and arcades below). Latrobe also sketched his version of a "principal building." It was larger in scale than the flanking Pavilions and topped with a dome.

Latrobe's influence was certainly greater than Thornton's although it's more difficult to assess. No less than seven of the Pavilions as built in the succeeding years would have colossal columns as Latrobe prescribed, an approach not previously favored by Jefferson. Two Pavilions are believed to have been based specifically on the long-promised Latrobe drawings that finally arrived on October 8, 1817; others may have been as well. Latrobe's finished drawings – probably arranged on one large sheet – almost certainly were beautiful, as Latrobe was an artist and watercolorist of great skill.

The content of that sheet and how much of it was incorporated into Jefferson's plan for the Academical Village remains a mystery since it disappeared long ago. The sheet's absence hasn't dampened speculation about precisely what was on it, as taking the measure of Latrobe's contribution to the process continues to be a source of lively debate (it has recently been suggested that a famous drawing of the Lawn from later in the construction process, long thought to have been done by Neilson, is actually the work of

The eastern façade of Hotel B with it's five-arch colonnade.

The famous "serpentine walls" define the gardens behind the Pavilions. Built of bricks and mortar, the curvilinear design actually saved material because the walls are only one brick thick but their undulating form gives them stability.

Latrobe). In any case, Latrobe is generally acknowledged to have been the earliest advocate for the idea of a principal building as well contributing designs for Pavilions III and IX. He proposed a "Center building which ought to exhibit in Mass & details as perfect a specimen of good Architectural taste as can be devised."

The craftsmen would make signal contributions, too. While Jefferson produced studies for each building that, in the tradition of Palladio's *Four Books*, combined the main elevation and floor plan on the same sheet, he did not execute detailed working drawings. His specifications for façades, and especially for exterior columns, cornice, and other classical details, were exacting; but details of interior finish were often left to the workmen. According to an 1819 advertisement in the Richmond *Enquirer*, builders would be required to provide their own working drawings for approval. That the tradesmen themselves contributed details is almost certain, as scholars have traced individual elements to pattern books not owned by Jefferson.

The cornerstone for Pavilion VII was laid on October 6, 1817, with President Monroe on hand, as well as his predecessors, Madison and Jefferson. The following June ground was broken for Pavilion III. But it was on January 25, 1819, that the Virginia General Assembly issued the charter for the University of Virginia, recognizing Charlottesville and the buildings at Central College as its home.

Although workmen were hired from Richmond and as far away as Philadelphia, construction proceeded at a Jeffersonian pace. Over the years some 200 workmen would be engaged in building the Village, many of them living in completed dormitory rooms, each of which had its own fireplace. A construction manager or "Proctor," Arthur S. Brockenbrough, was hired to relieve pressures on Jefferson and to expedite construction. By 1819 work on seven Pavilions had begun but the measured pace of the building – dictated, in part, by a lack of money – made impossible Jefferson's hope to welcome the first enrollees in 1820.

The plan had also grown more ambitious. In 1818 Jefferson had incorporated two dining halls ("Hotels") into the plan. In subsequent revisions the number would grow to six, with three aligned in each of two rows behind and parallel to the ten Pavilions. Jefferson dubbed the Hotels, together with additional dormitories linking them, the "East Range" and "West Range." The Ranges were set far enough behind the Pavilions to allow for generous gardens. By the summer of 1819, the plan called for these gardens to be enclosed by the memorable serpentine brick walls.

Jefferson's village, pictured here thirty years after his death, had changed little in the intervening years. The Rotunda, however, is notably out of scale, more than double its actual size, perhaps because when this 1856 lithograph was produced the new Annex wing to the rear engaged drafts-man Edward Sachse's eye. Thomas Jefferson Papers, The Albert and Shirley Small Special Collections Library, University of Virginia Library.

With an important assist from Latrobe, the Rotunda began to take shape, too. Just as he had done with his Richmond Capitol design, Jefferson became the medium for blending an anonymous work from antiquity with the work of a skilled contemporary architect. The model was the Pantheon (on the verso of his Rotunda drawing, Jefferson wrote that the diameter would be "77.feet, being ½ that of the Pantheon . . ."). As usual, Palladio was a silent presence, too, since Jefferson knew the Pantheon only from Palladio's *Four Books.*

While many architectural details are borrowed from the edition of Palladio Jefferson favored, the Pantheon in Rome had eight columns supporting its pediment, and the Jefferson-Latrobe version has only six. Latrobe must have given Jefferson some direction that led to this and other changes, since on his drawing of the Rotunda Jefferson inscribed on the top-right corner of the front elevation "Latrobe no. [illegible]," presumably a reference to Latrobe's master drawing. Amid Jefferson's specs on the back Latrobe's name appears again ("Latrobe's Rotunda, reduced to the proportion of the Pantheon . . . ."). Latrobe's presence may be palpable, but then Jefferson had conceived an early plan for the Capitol in Washington which was modeled on the Pantheon in Rome. It featured elliptical rooms, as

Jefferson trusted the purity of geometry (specifically a sphere, here on display) to endow his Rotunda with an austere beauty. Thomas Jefferson Papers, The Albert and Shirley Small Special Collections Library, University of Virginia Library.

does the Rotunda at the University. In retrospect, Jefferson's scheme for the U.S. Capitol looks like a fitting rehearsal for the Academical Village, and the Rotunda clearly reflects contributions from Latrobe, Palladio, and anonymous Roman architects, as well as Jefferson.

The Rotunda was begun in 1823, and was near enough to completion that the Marquis de Lafayette, taking his famous American tour, was fêted in the grand library room in 1824 by some 400 guests. But it was March 7, 1825, before the first forty students matriculated under the watchful eyes of five professors. Though the Rotunda remained unfinished when Jefferson died the following July, the number of enrollees had reached 180.

Jefferson's dream-come-true has seen its share of changes. The first major one was the Annex, an elongated wing built onto the back of the Rotunda in 1852. Designed by Jefferson's former draftsman, Robert Mills (best remembered for his design of the Washington Monument), the Annex housed classroom space and an auditorium that accommodated twelve hundred. The next major addition was a chapel completed after prolonged debate in 1889, and the Fayerweather Gymnasium that followed in 1893-94. Each of these buildings was sited just outside and north of the Jeffersonian precinct, which ran counter to Jefferson's vision that his University would expand southward along the established lines of the Pavilions and Hotels.

A fire on October 27, 1895 precipitated important changes on The Lawn. The Rotunda was reduced to a smoking hulk, and the partnership of Charles Follen McKim, William Mead, and Stanford White of New York was hired to rebuild. The firm attempted to honor Jefferson's intentions but, in keeping with the tenor of the time, did so confident that they could improve upon his vision. In recognition of the growth and reorientation of the campus, Stanford White, the partner in charge, designed a second, north-facing portico "similar to the one on the [south] front." He also eliminated the main level of elliptical rooms, transforming the library into a towering space.

White saw this as consistent with the original building. He termed the remodeled library a "deviation from the original plan . . . but . . . one which Jefferson would unquestionably have adopted . . . could he have directed the restoration." His assertion is dubious at best, though the resulting space was indisputably dramatic and its colossal Corinthian columns evocative of the Pantheon. White, however, cannot be saddled with all the blame for abandoning Jefferson's plan since the faculty had voted for such changes months before McKim, Mead, and White got the commission.

But White and company weren't finished. Over the next decade, they designed Carr's Hill, the president's manse, and Garrett Hall, a refectory, among other buildings. The firm prepared a master plan for future growth that was sympathetic to the Lawn, keeping Jefferson's buildings at the core while allowing for expansion with symmetrical courtyards to the south. But the first stage would be the addition of three new buildings that closed off the south end of the lawn.

Even today, emotions run high when the subject of Cabell, Rouss, and Cocke Halls is mentioned. This trio of buildings delimits the bounds of the Village. The vista of a distant horizon once defined by the mists of the Ragged Mountains has been foreshortened; the view became one of bricks and mortar, Stanford White style. Again, White needn't bear all the blame, as the Board of Visitors specified the site, and the new buildings were constructed to replace essential spaces such as lecture halls and laboratories lost in the Annex fire. Whether or not the closure of Jefferson's square diminished the Academical Village poses an important question, but the answer is strictly academic because the pastoral quality of Monroe Hill and environs can never be recaptured. Cabell, Rouss, and Cocke Halls screened not only the Ragged Mountains but a sprawling African-American neighborhood the Board of Visitors regarded as unsightly. The rolling countryside had already become part of a growing city.

The arcade beneath the Rotunda and its terraces, extending the width of The Lawn.

At about the time the McKim, Mead, and White association with the University was ending, Jefferson's architectural drawings were published in the landmark collection of 1916 edited by Fiske Kimball. In 1919, Kimball was hired to establish an architecture program at the University of Virginia as Jefferson had envisioned (its first headquarters was Hotel E on the West Range). Later Kimball became chair of the restoration committee at Monticello when the house entered the public trust in 1923. But it was Frederick Doveton Nichols, Kimball's heir as scholar-in-chief of Thomas Jefferson, Architect, who attempted to turn the clock back at the University.

The popular and influential Nichols, a professor at the School of Architecture, waged a twenty-year campaign to restore the Rotunda to its Jeffersonian appearance. He eventually prevailed and the McKim, Mead, and White interiors were removed in 1973. A best-guess version of Jefferson's design was installed in time for the nation's bicentennial celebration. This remodeling, too, has proved controversial and most preservationists today

Cabell Hall, a McKim, Mead, and White building (1896-98), could be the centerpiece at another university but is unremarkable in the context of the Jeffersonian Precinct. The building with its allegorical sculpture in the pediment (the theme is the Greek motto, "Ye Shall Know the Truth and the Truth Shall Make You Free"), feels two-dimensional. Jefferson's buildings are nothing if not bold; in comparison, this work of Stanford White seems elegant but meek.

feel strongly that the White renovation was too important to have been simply demolished, particularly given incomplete knowledge of Jefferson's original.

In the 1980s a less radical restoration was begun that is making its way around the Academical Village, one building at a time, restoring and preserving. After decades in which Jefferson's buildings were provided little more than basic maintenance, this new regime requires a comprehensive analysis of the history, condition, and usage of each building. The Jeffersonian Restoration Advisory Board was founded and the position of Architect for the Historic Buildings and Grounds established. The premise from the start was that Jefferson's intentions were to be honored – the Academical Village was not to be a museum but would remain at the heart of the University. Most of the Pavilions are now solely residential, though two again have classrooms, consistent with Jefferson's plans. But respecting the past and dealing with contemporary demands is an ongoing juggling act. While some of Jefferson's

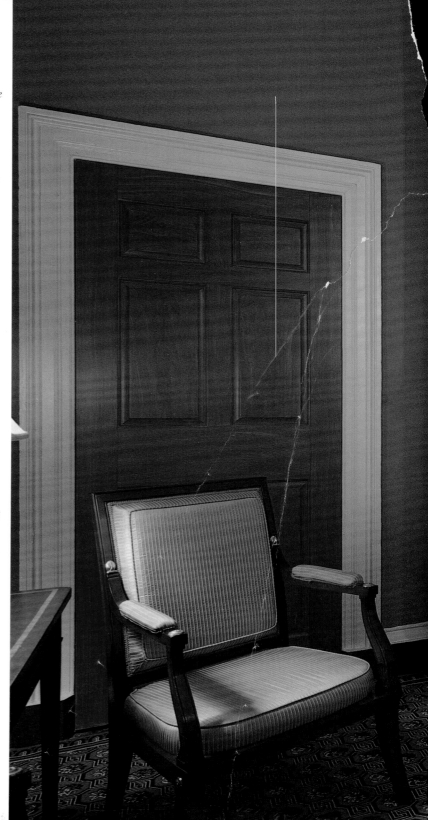

The interior of Pavilion VII has just been restored. Today it's the Colonnade Club for faculty and alumni.

original metal roofs, for example, have been restored, the Americans with Disabilities Act has required the addition of lifts and ramps to make buildings wheelchair accessible.

Remaking the past – even an important Jeffersonian past – is never a simple or straightforward matter.

Jefferson wrote that the creation of the University of the Virginia was "the last service that I can render my country." As such, it was a pubic project, intended to serve the commonweal for generations to come. At another moment he described the same undertaking as the "hobby of my old age," and establishing the University proved to be a profoundly personal process. The Academical Village, then, reflects the tastes of a private man able to express a larger vision his countrymen embraced as their own.

In planning not only the buildings but also the curriculum, library, and faculty, he envisioned a school unlike the one he had attended. William and Mary in his student days had been staffed almost entirely with clergymen but, as a secular man, Jefferson was determined that his university would have no professorship of divinity. He designed no chapel for his college; the building at the nucleus was a library. He saw that building as "a temple of knowledge," a place for books. He was no atheist, but for him the separation of church and state applied to public education. For Jefferson, learning and the written word were themselves hallowed.

The influence of classical authors he had studied and even of his revered Virginia are reflected in the composition of the Academical Village. Jefferson's political philosophy was essentially agrarian – he was suspicious of cities and often wrote and dreamt of a utopian place in which men lived off the land in perfect harmony. His

models were derived from classical authors like Horace and Cicero who had written of wise men living thoughtful lives in a pastoral mode. He looked, too, to Roman and Palladian villas, to New England villages, and even his own self-contained community at Monticello. He built a village of the mind, one after his own heart, with all the dignity and order (and orders) that classical architecture could bestow.

Jefferson's buildings at the University are his final statement on the art of architecture, but it is equally true that they represent a summing up of his earlier trials. A close examination of the Academical Village leaves one thinking of its allusions to the common sources from which Monticello, Poplar Forest, Barboursville, and the rest were drawn. The Rotunda with its dome, the hierarchy of orders, and the multiple patterns of Chippendale rails are all familiar. The colonnades are grand Palladian wings appended to the Rotunda in the manner of Monticello's dependencies. To walk The Lawn is a pleasure, but it's an especial joy for anyone conversant with the architectural manuals of the eighteenth century, as well as Jefferson's other architectural work. Taken together, the Pavilions con-

Jefferson played favorites — hilltops, for one, domes for another. Inside the Rotunda is this grand domed space with an oculus at its top that splashes light across the room as the sun traverses the sky.

Pairs of composite order columns define the inner perimeter of this multipurpose room. Like many domed spaces, the Rotunda has a "whispering gallery," in which a sotto voce *phrase uttered at one side of the dome's base is heard clearly 180 degrees away across the dome.*

stitute an open-book examination: the allusions to Roman ruins are all there, but expressed in a vernacular that Jefferson himself developed.

Today the Academical Village is a living place, a great, terraced expanse of green with the Rotunda dominating its north end. The timelessness of the place struck me on one

quiet October morning during the shooting of the photographs for this book. The Lawn wasn't overrun with frisbee-playing students as it often is (that's a use Jefferson could not have anticipated, but it animates the place on warm sunny days). The photographic conditions were perfect that morning, with the sun just peering over the East Range, casting long shadows that reached across the green. The hour was early — before seven o'clock — and the University was just awakening. A couple of dog walkers meandered through, and a vis-

If The Lawn makes one want to pull out his camera — and it does — then the gardens call for an easel and brushes to record the rich greens and explosion of colorful blooms.

When Jefferson planned the plots behind the pavilions, he envisioned them as productive gardens. Much later, beginning in 1948, the Garden Club of Virginia began underwriting the restoration of the gardens and the serpentine walls that enclose them. The three gardens in these images frame the rear façades of Pavilions VIII (facing page, bottom), VI (facing page, top), IV, respectively. The undulating brick walls hold implied promises, fulfilled by the lush gardens, with their parterres, draping ivy, sun dappling, and old and fragile trees.

iting dad with a camera walked by. Students living in the dormitories that enclose The Lawn began appearing in bathrobes, carrying their baskets of toiletries (no baths have been installed in the original dorm rooms). That Sunday the place had a morning-after feel, the Virginia Cavalier football team having been drubbed by Florida State the night before. There were a few beer cans, but not so many. Amid the veritable forest of classical columns, they almost didn't count.

The visual impact of Jefferson's Academical Village is a bit overwhelming. You take it in as best you can; analysis can come later. It's large in scale — twenty-odd major buildings, thirty-odd acres of tailored landscape — and it has a wonderful uniformity, the red masonry contrasting the bright white architectural details. But that morning it was the diversity that drew me.

I knew, of course, that no two buildings were alike, that that was a part of Jefferson's pedagogical master plan (he envisioned "models in architecture of the purest forms of antiquity, furnishing to the student examples of the precepts he will be taught in that art"). The columned arcades and porticoes contributed to a sense of continuity, yet that morning they seemed wildly varied, with Tuscan, Doric, Ionic, and Corinthian capitals, and a range of molding profiles, cornice details, frieze decorations, doorways, porches, and roof shapes. In the Roman encyclopedia before my eyes, I saw a place that manages to be both self-consciously derivative and wholly original. No mean trick, that.

The site, too, contributes in an important way to the uniqueness of the place. As my photographer colleague worked to capture the rosy glow of the sun that lit up the dome of the Rotunda, I walked to the south to the vista that once included Monticello at the horizon line. I turned back and looked north. The grade rises gently,

Jefferson based the façade of Pavilion I (it's Roman Doric, with bulky smooth columns) on plates of the ancient Baths of Diocletian in Rome in a book by sixteenth-century French architect Roland Fréart de Chambray. It was built by two gifted Jefferson builders, namely James Oldham, carpenter, who had begun working for Jefferson at Monticello, and William Phillips, mason, who would be building Jeffersonian Classical courthouses for decades to come. Thomas Jefferson Papers, The Albert and Shirley Small Special Collections Library, University of Virginia Library.

The cornice on Pavilion II (left) is adapted from Palladio (who had recorded and drawn the Roman temple of Fortuna Virilis). The Ionic capitals were carved in Italy of Carrara marble, and delivered to Charlottesville by boat and oxcart. The balcony on this, as with several other pavilions, was suspended from iron rods, a structural solution that Jefferson had observed on his travels.

The second Pavilion to be constructed, Pavilion III (top right), was begun in 1818. The builders were Monticello veteran John Dinsmore, carpenter, and mason John Perry, who had worked at both of Jefferson's homes, along with Perry's brother Rueben.

The design was a Latrobe-Jefferson collaboration, based initially on a sketch from Latrobe's sheet of drawings. It appears, however, to have been Jefferson's notion to compress the columns, resulting in a dramatic contrast to the other Pavilions fronted with four columns, such as Pavilion IV (left) which, begun a year later, faces it across The Lawn.

Pavilion VI is the simplest of the Pavilions, with comparatively small windows and a one-story porch. Yet it's an elegant building, with a plain but stately Tuscan colonnade and Roman Ionic details from the Theater of Marcellus in Rome.

The lineage at Pavilion VIII is traced to Latrobe (Jefferson notes in his specification books regarding this Pavilion, "Latrobe's Lodge front"). It faces the Thornton-inspired Pavilion VII across the lawn. Jefferson designed the building with a flat roof fronted by a parapet but leaks developed so a hip roof was later added. For many years Pavilion VIII served as the president's offices, but after a recent restoration, the ground floor rooms have been returned to Jefferson's intended use — once again professors conduct classes in Pavilion VIII, as well as in Pavilion V.

Over the years, the design of Pavilion IX has been variously attributed – it's Jefferson, of course, as this drawing (left) was executed on his drawing board. But he may have been under the spell of the French Neoclassicists Étienne-Louis Boullée and Claude-Nicholas Ledoux (and specifically, the latter's Hôtel de Mlle Guimard). The niche doorway (above) was once interpreted as evidence of that, although recent scholarship suggests that the idea was Latrobe's (the latter's name, in Jefferson's hand, appears on his drawing) and is likely to have been based on ancient Roman sources as well as on later French ones. What isn't in dispute, however, is how alive the entrance is as the sun explores its contours. Thomas Jefferson Papers, The Albert and Shirley Small Special Collections Library, University of Virginia Library.

Pavilion X was the work of master craftsman John Neilson whose genius is in evidence not only at Monticello but at Bremo (see page 172) and the Rotunda. Jefferson's design is an amalgam of the Roman, as it is loosely based on the Doric order at the Theater of Marcellus, and the Greek as Jefferson, in a bow to Hellenic models, instructed that the columns be built with no bases.

The Anatomical Theatre was built when Dr. Robley Dunglison, professor of Anatomy and Medicine, complained that the combined home and class-room space in his designated Pavilion X was ill-suited for the teaching of anatomy, which involved the dissection of cadavers. Jefferson obliged with a design, the Board of Visitors the funding, and the building was executed (though it was unfinished at Jefferson's death in 1826). It was sited outside the Academical Village, a utilitarian afterthought, and lacked the careful classicism of the rest of Jefferson's University. The Anatomical Theater was demolished in 1939 and the new library constructed in its place. Thomas Jefferson Papers, The Albert and Shirley Small Special Collections Library, University of Virginia Library.

the terraces ascending to the steps of the Rotunda. The wide, grassy commons that climb the hill were the work of men with shovels; I wondered if, had he today's earthmoving equipment, would Jefferson have flattened the site? Stanford White probably would have thought so, I mused, and at the thought of White, I turned back to the south to look upon his three buildings. They seemed too cool, too regular, the moldings too small. The McKim, Mead, and White buildings aren't as bold as Jefferson's, and that morning I saw them as too tight, overly controlled. There's a luscious quality of Jefferson's quadrangle that contrasts to the sterility of Cabell, Rouss, and Cocke halls at its end.

If Monticello was Jefferson's apprenticeship, then the University of Virginia was his masterwork. Monticello may be more personal – certainly, it is his most autobiographical work, as one can read the events of his life in its evolution – but his University reflects the public man. The buildings he designed at the University of Virginia are an embodiment of his larger vision for Virginia and America. He saw an essential link between democracy and education, between an educated populace and good governance. The buildings he designed at the University of Virginia are a blend of his vision and a disciplined collation of what he liked from the classical past.

For the expert, the interested amateur, and even for those who don't know the Ionic from the ironic, a visit to the Academical Village is among the greatest – some say *the* greatest – of American architectural experiences.

A life-size statue of Mr. Jefferson stands on the main floor of the Rotunda, framed by the vast curving staircases leading to the dome room above. Sculpted by Alexander Galt in 1860, the sculpture was saved by students from the fire of 1895.

The Jeffersonian Legacy

"Directly or indirectly American classicism traces its ancestry to Jefferson, who may truly be called the father of our national architecture."
— Fiske Kimball,
Thomas Jefferson, Architect, 1916

When Thomas Jefferson began building Monticello, Charlottesville was a town in name only. Some of the plantations in the surrounding countryside looked more like villages than Charlottesville did since the county seat for Albemarle County consisted of nothing more than a fifty-acre grid of undeveloped land with a courthouse, a tavern, and a handful of houses. By the time its most prominent citizen died more than half a century later, however, Charlottesville had become a burgeoning town.

McKim, Mead and White's president's house, Carr's Hill (1907-09) at the University of Virginia.

The place had also assumed a distinctly Jeffersonian character. Even today Jefferson's long shadow dominates the landscape in a way that cannot be explained solely by reference to his home or even the style-book array of classical buildings at the Academical Village. Jefferson's architectural influence outlived him, possessed of an unstoppable momentum provided by a small army of builders.

He had lamented in his book *Notes on the State of Virginia* in 1781 that "a workman could scarcely be found here capable of drawing an order." By the time he died on July 4, 1826, he had single-handedly effected a reversal. The builders he had schooled at Monticello, Poplar Forest, and the University of Virginia continued to work in Albemarle and the surrounding counties after the great man's death. As builders in any era will do, they built what they knew, producing hundreds of well-made buildings, many in the idiom we know as Jeffersonian Classicism. Tetrastyle porticoes (porches with four columns across the front), lunettes in pediments, symmetrical Palladian plans, Chippendale railings, triple-sash windows, and other elements drawn from the works of Jefferson became the local vernacular. And the work consisted of more than houses. Civic buildings, especially for the courts, were built by Jefferson's builders all over Virginia, at least one of them to a design by Jefferson himself (see page 179). His symbolic use of classical sources in the Virginia Capitol and his influence upon design in Washington, D.C., helped inspire countless buildings in other states, too.

When Jefferson had begun sketching Monticello, his genteel Virginia neighbors were building Georgian homes based on English models, and not so many years after his death the Greek Revival superceded his style as the mode of the moment, with designs derived from popular plan books by such architect-authors as Asher Benjamin and Minard Lafever. But in the decades between, there was Jefferson, an otherwise Protean figure who, in alternate moments, worked at being a philosopher, politician, scientist, farmer, and educator. But as an architect his legacy is a coherent style that defined a region.

Though almost none are by Jefferson, the buildings in this chapter all are recognizably Jeffersonian. They are major buildings constructed by the masons and carpenters who had worked for Jefferson, men who learned his style first-hand. James Dinsmore and John Neilson appear here, along with a host of talented others, including John M. Perry, William B. Phillips, Malcolm F. Crawford, and George Wilson Spooner, Jr. The stories and images of their works make a primae facie case for Jefferson's standing as the American architect who more than any other – more than the inimitable Wright, more than H.H. Richardson or Stanford White or the rest – so perfectly understood the practical and philosophical needs of his countrymen that, at least in Jefferson country, his style came to seem inevitable.

First we'll follow the footsteps of James Dinsmore and John Neilson, undoubtedly the most gifted of Jefferson's builders. According to an entry in Jefferson's journal for April 19, 1809, "Dinsmore and Neilson are set out yesterday for Montpelier." Between them they had fifteen years of experience helping Jefferson realize his vision of Monticello.

The next stop on their architectural travels was the home of the new president, James Madison. The building chronology there is complicated, since the original structure was built by the future president's father circa 1760 and the younger Madison, who was among Jefferson's most trusted friends and political allies, had previously consulted Jefferson around 1797. At that time Montpelier was enlarged and had a look-at-me portico applied. By 1809 the time had come to make the house more presidential and, at Jefferson's suggestion, Neilson and Dinsmore arrived to help.

Given its date of initial construction, **MONTPELIER** could hardly be pure Jefferson. In fact, it isn't pure anything today, having been home to three generations of Madisons and, in the twentieth century, to several generations of

MONTPELIER, VA

the Seat of the late James Madison.

Madison's Montpelier, in an 1836 engraving. Jefferson consulted on the portico though the tempietto, the garden folly to the left, is thought to have been built by Neilson and Dinsmore to a plan by Dr. William Thornton. The Library of Virginia.

DuPonts, the last of whom bequeathed it to the National Trust. The house today is immense, thanks to multiple, grand, Colonial Revival additions from the DuPont years. But there remains a kernel of Madison to which Dinsmore and Neilson, as well as another stalwart Jefferson worker, Hugh Chisolm, also contributed. But these Jefferson workers would soon produce other, more original works.

Bremo remains the property of Cocke descendants and remarkably unchanged aside from a reconfiguration of the roof in the General's lifetime. These images date from a recording of the house done by the Historic American Building Survey in 1940. HABS/Library of Congress.

❖

Sometimes the pupil outperforms the professor, and there are those who believe that John Neilson did just that at **UPPER BREMO**, the house he constructed between 1817 and 1820.

Today the Bremo Historic District in Fork Union, Fluvanna County, consists of three estates, Upper Bremo, Lower Bremo, and Bremo Recess. All were properties of General John Hartwell Cocke, who earned his rank in the War of 1812. It is Upper Bremo (called hereafter Bremo) that has an important yet ambiguous place in the Jefferson canon.

Thomas Jefferson, Architect, did not design Bremo, although in the past the house was credited to him by such knowledgeable scholars as Fiske Kimball. While Jefferson's direct role in the design was small, it is perhaps more than fair to think of Bremo as an adoptive child of his.

The Palladian barn at Bremo is unique. Built prior to the mansion, the barn was a training exercise. The construction of its field-stone columns and various arch configurations was surely excellent experience for Virginia builders largely unfamiliar with classical architecture. HABS/Library of Congress.

One of the designers was certainly Cocke himself, and a variety of friends and relations are known to have influenced preliminary plans, among them his wife, Ann Barraud Cocke. When General Cocke sought Jefferson's help, he got some excellent guidance but not a design per se. Jefferson offered his oft-quoted "let-Palladio-be-your-Bible" remark but resisted the tempting commission because he felt acutely the absence of his essential reference books, having just sold his library to the nation. He also urged Cocke to hire builders from his personal stable, so Cocke enlisted John Neilson. Jefferson's surrogate became undertaker for Bremo and, along with Cocke, gets principle credit for this extraordinary house. The cornerstone at Bremo reflects the extent of his contribution, identifying him as architect of Bremo.

In examining Neilson's surviving drawings, it is apparent both that he was Jefferson's superior as a draftsman and that he improved upon the design that Cocke *et al.* had developed. In plan the house is Jeffersonian-Palladian, with obvious similarities to both Monticello and Palladio's Villa Emo. The main house is flanked by two pavilions connected by long dependencies submerged into the hillside. Inside the house the arrangement of rooms, passages, and stairs suggest a Jeffersonian plan. Many details also seem to have come from the same source, including the foreshortening of first- and second-story windows into what appears to be one unit; precise classical detailing on the exterior and interior; and many characteristically Jeffersonian conveniences such as bed alcoves, a rotating pantry door, and suppressed stairs.

Again, Jefferson didn't design this house. Nor, by the same token, did his stand-in, John Neilson, do it alone. But the ironic result of the confab of family, friends, and builders is a house that, as more than one wag has remarked, seems more Jefferson than Jefferson. Whether or not it's the most perfectly realized house in the Jefferson idiom will long be debated, but the line of transmission – from Palladio to Jefferson to Neilson – is indisputable.

The central block at Estouteville consists of two tall stories and, together with its wings, the building extends 152 feet.

If Bremo was John Neilson's finest independent work, then **ESTOUTEVILLE** was James Dinsmore's. By the time he designed and built this house between 1827 and 1830, Dinsmore had spent two decades working for Jefferson. He had been hired by him in 1798 and remained at Monticello until April of 1809 when he departed for Montpelier. Though he purchased a sawmill and speculated in real estate in Charlottesville, a few years later he was once again at work for Jefferson, this time at the University. He and Neilson built the Rotunda, the Anatomical Theater, and at least three pavilions and fourteen dormitory rooms.

The agreement between owner Philip Barbour and builder John Perry specified that, at Frascati, "The brick work [is] to be the equal to any . . . at the University." Jefferson had set the standard.

Colonel John Coles III owned the Estouteville property, a large plantation near Powell Corner in Albemarle County that, by the Civil War era, would expand to 11,500 contiguous acres. He hired Dinsmore to build him a suitable mansion house, and he got what he asked for, as Estouteville is stately and monumental. The Jeffersonian borrowings are obvious from first glance: Roman revival porticos dominate both façades, and the main hall inside is decorated with an academically correct cornice adapted from Palladio's *Four Books*. Another veteran builder from the University, William B. Philips, was the principal mason.

Estouteville stands as a testament to Jefferson's belief that stylish buildings will beget other quality buildings – this style book-perfect example of Virginia classicism would not look as it does without the Jefferson connection. In a quirk of fate, Dinsmore probably never saw Estouteville completed as he drowned in the Rivanna River in May of 1830.

Another alumnus of Monticello and Poplar Forest was John M. Perry, who built **FRASCATI** between 1821-23, simultaneous to his labors for Jefferson at the University. Although he knew Jefferson's design inclinations from first-hand experience, this house is an intriguing mixture. Located in Somerset, Orange County, Frascati is a conservative, boxy, five-bay

Georgian style house, with various Federal details drawn from one of the most popular building books of the day, *The American Builder's Companion* (first edition, 1806) by Asher Benjamin.

The owner of the house was Colonel Philip Pendleton Barbour, brother of Governor James Barbour of Barboursville (see page 112) and himself a U.S. Supreme Court justice. Jefferson knew both Barbours and had even designed Barboursville for James, but the well documented Frascati was not his work. Still, the character of its façade is certainly determined by the monumental portico – with its Tuscan columns and detailing, it's distinctly Jeffersonian.

John Perry appeared earlier in this book. An intriguing character, he was both a master carpenter and brick mason, having been the head carpenter for the first building at the University, Pavilion VII, and later principal mason at three other Pavilions and two of the hotels. He was also an accomplished iron worker. He had dabbled in real estate, buying and selling a number of properties, and owned a lumber mill, at least thirty-seven slaves, and a considerable library. He became a magistrate and later, as a justice of the peace, appraised Jefferson's estate.

In the did-he-or-didn't-he debate, the answer at **AMPTHILL** is a definite maybe. Jefferson probably did have a hand in the design of the house, even if none of his builders did.

The building was built about 1835. Any architectural historian seeking to classify it would identify the house as an example of Jeffersonian Classicism by virtue of Ampthill's single-story design, red brick envelope with tall trim windows and white marble lintels, and the bold four-columned portico. (For the record, it should be noted that Ampthill is actually two houses connected by a short passage, with an original eighteenth century wood-frame home almost hidden behind the later brick structure.)

The property was once part of Clifton, an immense eighteenth-century plantation owned by the Carter family in Cumberland County. Originally known as The Fork, the property became Ampthill at the time the Jeffersonian addition was built. The property had been owned in successive generations by members of the Carter and Randolph families before coming into the hands of Randolph Harrison, whose mother had been Susannah Randolph, a sister of Thomas Jefferson's mother, Jane. In September 1815 the former president wrote a letter to Randolph Harrison that is the best evidence of his role in designing the home.

"During a long visit to this place," Jefferson reported, "I have had leisure to think of your house. You seem to require six rooms, neither more nor less, and a good entrance or passage of communication. The enclosed is drawn on that plan. The ground plan is in detail and exact, the elevation merely a sketch to give a general idea. The workman, if he is anything of an architect, will be able to draw the particulars." Family history has it that Harrison began to build the house only after his wife's death some twenty years later because he believed a new stylish house would be attractive to the younger woman he was courting.

Jefferson's drawings have been lost, but their vagueness ("merely a sketch") is consistent with the look of the house. The façade lacks the symmetry that Jefferson preferred. The moldings aren't Roman but Greek, no doubt attributable to a change in fashion and a popular builder's book titled *Practical House Carpenter* by Asher Benjamin published in 1830. Many details in the house were copied from its plates, in particular mantels installed to update fireplaces in the existing wood-frame house. Diluted Jefferson it may be, but even at first glance Ampthill's patrimony seems apparent.

❧ FOLLY ❧

This house has many of the qualifications. Like most Jefferson designs, it features porticos with lunette windows and four Tuscan columns each, as well as a symmetrical plan on a raised basement. Other details, too, could have been drawn from Mr. Jefferson's bag of architectural tricks and, very likely, they were. Only not by Jefferson.

The temptation to add Folly to the list of Jefferson's works is great. The timing is right, as Folly was built between 1818 and 1820. There's also a strong resemblance between Folly and Edgemont, both of which have nearly square plans and multiple porticos (see page 97). Then there's the serpentine wall that encloses a garden on the approach to Folly.

Folly has remained in the possession of the original builder's descendants. It is Joseph Smith's great, great, great-grandson who is Folly's caretaker today. While the family inheritance is thoroughly documented, no direct connection to Jefferson has been established. He is unlikely to have designed the house; there is no evidence even that any of his many builders contributed. And certain details of the building itself belie the attribution. The window trim and cornice details, for example, more nearly resemble plates in plan books of the time than Jefferson's designs.

Still, the house does suggest that Jefferson's ideas were well known and admired. Even today the house seems perfectly suited to its little rise, surrounded by substantial acreage that remains from its days as a plantation, with its glorious view of the Shenandoah Valley less than hour west of Charlottesville.

In the past, the claim was often made that this serpentine wall predated those at Mr. Jefferson's university, though today there seems to be general accord among architectural historians that Folly's walls were inspired by rather than the inspiration for the curvilinear walls in Charlottesville. Though in somewhat deteriorated condition — such walls are only one brick wide and have minimal footers — Folly's wall is largely original, unlike those at the University which have been rebuilt.

This low-lying house is one story tall, with a hip roof that enhances its horizontal appearance. The most surprising element in a Jeffersonian Classical house, however, is that Ampthill is asymmetrical, with three window bays on the left and two to the right of the portico.

❖

Venerable Virginia houses with names like Berry Hill, Esmont, Westend, East Belmont, Oak Lawn, Stono, and Willow Grove all have vague connections to Jefferson, typically having been built by men who worked for him at Monticello or the Academical Village, which together must be regarded as among America's most influential building academies. During his presidency, James Monroe sought his old friend's advice before building his private residence, Oak Hill, between 1820 and 1823. There are innumerable more modest houses in the Central Virginia countryside that were built (or remodeled) after Jefferson's time that have characteristic Jeffersonian details.

He helped establish a building culture in Virginia which produced not only houses but courthouses. A dozen or more county court houses in Virginia are notably Jeffersonian, although the man himself actually assisted in designing no more two or three of them. He probably contributed a plan for the Botetourt County court house in 1818, despite the fact the structure that stands today isn't remotely Jeffersonian (it was built some twenty years later in a Greek Revival style and subsequently burned and was rebuilt). But court houses in Charlotte and Buckingham Counties may have been built to a plan Jefferson provided in 1821 or 1822.

An unnamed drawing in Jefferson's hand survives. For many years it was believed to be the plan for the **BUCKINGHAM COUNTY COURTHOUSE** and that the **CHARLOTTE COURTHOUSE** had been subsequently copied from the Buckingham building. The case was made on the basis of correspondence between Jefferson and Colonel Charles Yancey, a

The influence spiraled out. This house, Morea, was built for John Patton Emmet. He had been one of the first eight faculty members Jefferson hired at his University (Emmet was Professor of Natural History) and initially resided in Pavilion I. By 1835 he had moved a short distance away to Morea which had been built, he wrote, to a plan "contrived by myself."

commissioner in charge of the court house project in Maysville, Buckingham County. An exchange of letters had induced Jefferson, as he said in his note of July 23, 1821, to send Yancey "the drawings you desired."

The courthouse at Buckingham was destroyed in 1869, so no physical evidence exists to support the attribution. More recently, however, an examination of the Charlotte County Courthouse has revealed it so closely resembles the drawing that it is now thought to have been Jefferson's prototype, with its bold temple front and lunette window in the pediment. The recent investigation also revealed the remains of foundations beneath a later addition to the rear that indicate the original footprint of the building was semi-octagonal, just as Jefferson had envisioned it.

Veteran University builders like Dabney Cosby, Sr., William B. Phillips, and Malcolm F. Crawford are connected to court houses in Cumberland, Goochland, Greene, Halifax, Lunenberg, Madison, Mecklenburg, Page, Sussex, and other counties. Jefferson's belief was that the citizens of the youthful American republic ought to be informed and edified by its public buildings; since these courthouses were central to public life in Virginia communities in the early nineteenth century, Jefferson would no doubt have been pleased to learn that in the years after his death so many court houses were built in the classical image he favored.

Above: Jefferson's floor plan for the Charlotte County Court House. Courtesy of the Massachusetts Historical Society.

The Charlotte County Court House (top left) was probably designed by Jefferson, while the court houses in Nottoway and Madison Counties were not. Yet there's a school-of-Jefferson feel to all three. The Madison County Courthouse (completed 1830; left) was built by William B. Phillips and Malcolm F. Crawford, both University builders. The Nottoway County Court House (1843, far left), has a three-part Palladian plan, with its central block and matching wings.

Though not a work of Jefferson's, the Christ Episcopal Church, Glendower, is a modest one-story parish church located a few miles south of Monticello. It was built by another builder experienced in the ways of Jefferson, William B. Phillips. Despite its rural setting, Christ Church, Glendower, is anything but rustic — it's pristine Jeffersonian Classical, with its Doric entablature and pleasing proportions.

The second home at **EDGEHILL** belonged to Thomas Jefferson Randolph (1792-1875), Jefferson's favorite grandson. The first Edgehill house had been designed by Jefferson for his daughter, Martha, and her husband Thomas Mann Randolph, (see page 107). Jeff, as the grandson was called, had bought the property at a debtor's auction in 1826 at which his own father's slaves and land were sold.

The main house on the property today was built in 1828 atop the foundations of the earlier home which had been moved to the rear of the property. Thomas Jefferson, Architect, probably had no direct role in this house, although in the past Fiske Kimball (as well as Jefferson descendants) asserted the building "was probably after a Jefferson design." In the absence of documentary evidence, there are some common characteristics, among them the Chinese lattice railing. But this is a stolid house with blocky proportions unrelieved by the lightness Jefferson typically brought to his designs.

While Jefferson did not contribute to the design of the 1828 Edgehill, his influence was certainly felt. Not only had the owner of the home spent countless hours in his grandfather's company, but the men Jeff Randolph hired to build the house had also come under Jefferson's tutelage. Edgehill's masonry columns are virtually identical to the Tuscan order columns that make up the colonnade surrounding The Lawn at the University.

CHRIST EPISCOPAL CHURCH

Thomas Jefferson apparently never designed a church although Christ Episcopal of Charlottesville was for many years thought to be his work. When Episcopal rector Reverend Frederick W. Hatch arrived in 1820, the Presbyterians, Baptists, Methodists, and Episcopalians met in the courthouse for services. Hatch set about changing that and at least one member of Hatch's con-

gregation, namely Thomas Jefferson, was quick to pledge twenty dollars a year to the building program. Over the next several years he would contribute 1,200 bricks and a subscription of $285.

In 1824, Hatch asked Jefferson for a plan but Jefferson was ailing so he turned to his trusted builder John Neilson, then still at work at the University. Neilson obliged with a sheet of drawings that survive. Neilson's design appears to have been too expensive, as a simpler building was erected. The builders and presumed designers were other Jeffersonians, John Perry and George W. Spooner, Jr., both of whom were then at work on the University. Construction began in 1824, and by the following year the red brick church was completed.

So, no, it is not a Jefferson building. By the time Fiske Kimball made a case in 1923 that it might be, the building was gone. Today only the original thirty-five-foot wide stone foundation survives in the basement of a newer structure.

The Christ Episcopal Church of Charlottesville in a nineteenth-century photograph. The church was demolished in 1895 to make way for a larger Gothic Revival church. Thomas Jefferson Papers, The Albert and Shirley Small Special Collections Library, University of Virginia Library.

Thomas Jefferson Randolph's Edgehill, built 1828, has been attributed to mason William B. Phillips and carpenter Malcolm F. Crawford, both of whom had worked at the University of Virginia and who continued thereafter to build in a Jeffersonian style.

The subsequent history of the house has been checkered. Martha Jefferson Randolph, widowed the same year the second Edgehill house was completed, had gone to Boston to live with a daughter. Shortly before her death in 1836, she returned to Shadwell to reside with her son, Jeff, at Edgehill. The house burned to a masonry shell in 1916 and was rebuilt thereafter, but by then it had fulfilled the important role it was to play in the history of Jefferson's architecture.

In his will, the former president had bequeathed his business and personal papers to Thomas Jefferson Randolph. Edgehill thus became an essential link with Jefferson as the repository for his papers. In the nineteenth century, many Jefferson documents were sold to the Department of State (in that era the Library of Congress, its role defined by its name, made no effort to collect presidential papers). Apparently the architectural drawings were of little interest, and they were forgotten in Edgehill's attic for many years. They passed from Jeff to his daughter, Mrs. Mary Walker Randolph, and a grand-daughter, Miss Cornelia J. Taylor. Then a Boston relation, another great-great-grand-child of Thomas Jefferson's, arrived in Virginia in 1911.

Thomas Jefferson Coolidge, Jr. (1863-1912) had had his curiosity about his ancestor's architecture piqued by a personal project of his. He had built himself a modified Monticello in Manchester, Massachusetts, a wealthy coastal town north of Boston. He had worked from measurements of the original Monticello, but was unaware of the existence of Jefferson's original drafts. The Edgehill cache was a major find. Even though the drawings had sustained water and mice damage over the decades, they were largely intact when Coolidge deposited them at the Massachusetts Historical Society, where the collection remains to this day.

While this may sound like the end of a story, it's actually a new beginning.

A century ago, Jefferson's architectural legacy was largely unknown. Biographies of the man made only passing mention of Monticello (which was then a private home in a state of advanced deterioration) and said nothing at all of his other building activities. Quite by accident Stanford White had seen a few of Jefferson's drawings for his University, but until 1913 there wasn't so much as a monograph devoted to Thomas Jefferson, Architect. The general public didn't learn of Jefferson's architecture until the Coolidge collection of his drawings was published in 1916.

Sidney Fiske Kimball (1888-1955) proved to be the medium for reintroducing the world to Thomas Jefferson's architectural accomplishments. Having recently earned his master's degree in architecture at Harvard, Kimball was at work on a history of architecture for New York publisher Harper & Brothers. As the story goes, his wife of only a few months found the words "Jefferson as an Architect" scrawled on piece of paper in her husband's hand in the summer of 1913. Marie Goebel Kimball began the research but by 1914 Fiske, too, was fully engaged and an article bearing his byline, "Thomas Jefferson as Architect: Monticello and Shadwell," was published in the *Architectural Quarterly*.

That same year Kimball happened across a reference to the Massachusetts Historical Society collection and was astounded at his good fortune. "It was marvelous," he remembered. "There were three or four hundred drawings. . . . They constituted a

The front elevation of Shack Mountain is pleasing in part because of the semi-octagonal ends that soften the box. The columns are unpretentious Tuscan, the windows triple-hung, the portico tetrastyle . . . all which has begun to sound happily familiar, perhaps?

wilderness of the most obscure kind. There was scarcely a signature in the lot, rarely any title, and but few dates." For a scholar of Kimball's immense energy, this was nothing short of an invitation, and within weeks he had gotten himself appointed editor of a memorial publication underwritten by the widow of Thomas Jefferson Coolidge, Jr., to commemorate his recent passing.

The publication of Fiske Kimball's *Thomas Jefferson, Architect* was a revelation. Nearly a century after its release, however, that imposing folio must be seen in the same way one regards the first map of a region. The Kimballs' accom-

The parlor at Shack Mountain is a tall and gracious room with a deep and imposing cornice. Note, too, the quarter-round parlor walls and the medallion of Jefferson, by sculptor Walter Hancock, above the dining room doorway.

plishments were formidable, as Marie Kimball examined some 40,000 Jefferson letters and documents, seeking references to his architecture. Fiske Kimball then pieced together a careful overview of Jefferson's architectural *oeuvre*, collating the words with the drawings. He immediately recognized from the drawings that Monticello had two radically different incarnations, the one that survived and Monticello I, the first version subsumed by Monticello II. From today's vantage, we can identify a few detours and cul-de-sacs that waylaid Kimball, but despite minor errors and missteps, his book is a monumental work. It contains facsimile reproductions of the Jefferson drawings in the Coolidge collection together with Kimball's text. The book remains the essential guide to which all scholars must refer.

Kimball marshaled his arguments and concluded his persuasive case with this: "Directly or indirectly American classicism traces its ancestry to Jefferson, who may truly be called the father of our national architecture."

Thomas Jefferson Coolidge, Jr., was far from the only person who wanted his own Monticello. Fiske Kimball was another, and he built a small-scale version four miles northwest of the University of Virginia in 1935-36.

He chose a Jeffersonian site, a ridge with a panoramic view. The house soon was dubbed **SHACK MOUNTAIN**, after the Shackelford family who had previously owned the property. The house Kimball designed was *T*-shaped, with the two principal rooms, a dining room and parlor, extending across the elongated octagon that forms the axis of the front façade. In an ell to the rear a kitchen, bedrooms, and a study completed the leg of the tee.

Unlike Monticello, Shack Mountain is truly a one-story house. It's a pavilion, built as a vacation and retirement home for the childless Kimballs. The Roman and Jeffersonian sources can be read as if from a check list, ranging from the Tuscan columns to the floor plan, which is a reprise of Jefferson's design for Farmington (see pages 106 and 108). But this house is much more than a Jeffersonian miniature.

Upon seeing Shack Mountain, Sir Kenneth Clarke rhapsodized, "It's a temple in the woods." Another critic described Shack Mountain as "a masterpiece of scale, setting, and reinterpretation." It has been called "a miniature Monticello," "gem-like," and a "tour-de-force." I like to think of it as distilled Jefferson, an essence infused with his ideas and spirit.

The dining room at Shack Mountain is filled with light thanks to the triple-hung Jeffersonian windows.

By editing and identifying Jefferson's drawings, Fiske Kimball made it possible to visit Jefferson's architectural "practice" (it was never a practice, of course, it was a hobby, an avocation). By introducing us to Jefferson's drawings he afforded us a rare opportunity to see the way in which the designers of the time worked to resolve architectural riddles – Jefferson left site plans, floor plans, elevations, details, even specifications from an era when master builders usually doubled as their own designers and standard practice was to work from nothing more than the most rudimentary of renderings.

Kimball's Shack Mountain has a status of its own. I've visited Shack Mountain several times and the place always leaves me thinking, admiring, wondering. The house is not a seminal work of twentieth-century architecture; it's grand but practical, solemn yet witty, erudite but unpretentious. Still, Shack Mountain will never be more than an intriguing footnote in the much larger Jefferson saga. After all, the house is an obvious act of homage to Jefferson.

Yet it was also an out-and-out rejection of modernism when Kimball's was a voice in the wilderness. At the very time Shack Mountain was designed and built, the Jeffersonian idiom was distinctly *outré*. Modernism was the vogue and

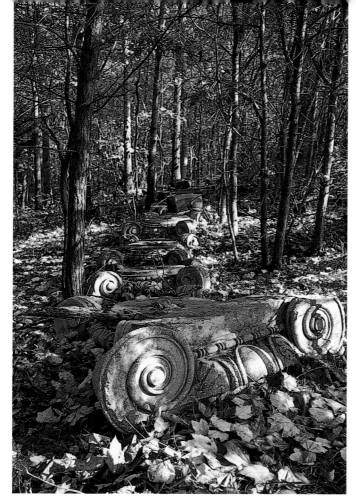

A ruin atop Shack Mountain?

even the notion of building the Jefferson Monument in Washington in a classical style was derided as degraded and irrelevant (John Russell Pope's monument took almost a decade to complete, and even then was significantly altered and roundly booed). But that makes Shack Mountain all the more important, a harbinger that traditional architecture had an enduring appeal. In that sense, Shack Mountain anticipates Postmodernism by half a century.

A few years ago, the present owner of Shack Mountain bought some architectural elements from the University. They had sat in a field near the school for years when she noticed a newspaper advertisement saying the pieces were for sale. As instructed, she submitted a sealed bid and soon received notification that the miscellaneous capitols and plinths were hers. She arranged for them to be moved to the edge of the forest at Shack Mountain, beyond the meadow north of the house. There they remain, obscured by brush growing on the forest floor. Perhaps some future architectural historian or archaeologist will be fooled into thinking that a temple once stood near Mr. Kimball's house. Then, perhaps, a wiser person will come along, as Sidney Fiske Kimball did, and explain what exactly it is they have found.

If the modernists were trying to purge the past from their minds – and many said they were – then Jefferson's (and Kimball's) attitude offers an important contrast. Jefferson liked nothing better than looking back. He learned much of what he knew from books about antique architecture; later, he saw looking-backward architecture in Paris, too. If Jefferson's buildings have an undeniable sameness about them, one can also see that as a wonderful constancy. He honed and polished, learned and improved; he was satisfied with achieving a mastery of his style. For him architecture was a pleasure; he had nothing to prove. Just as important, he had no paying client to please. He was free to do what he wanted, within certain financial constraints and the limitations imposed by his rural outpost with its shortfall of skilled labor and of certain materials. At Monticello, in particular, he integrated his whims and wishes, his conveniences and modern contrivances. But above all, as Fiske Kimball reminded us, Jefferson linked us to the past.

Afterword

"If Inigo Jones was called Vitruvius Britannicus, most meetly are you to be handed the laurels as Vitruvius Americanus."
– John Rowley, British guest at Monticello

Thanks to Fiske Kimball and a host of others, Thomas Jefferson, Architect, has emerged from obscurity. Today schoolchildren are taught that this patriot president was America's first great native-born architect. He was an architectural reformer who saw the vernacular architecture of Virginia and colonial America as debased. He sought to reform tastes, to bring to the new

Thomas Sully was commissioned to paint this portrait to hang at West Point. He spent twelve days at Monticello in 1821 and was said to have "left the place with great reluctance." Although nearly seventy-eight years old, Jefferson stands nearly as firm and straight as the column next to him, yet with an unpretentious ease. The original painting is more than eight feet tall. West Point Museum Collection, United States Military Academy.

nation the virtues of classical architecture which involved the use of architectural orders, and his campaign certainly succeeded. While he was a public man with republican goals, he was also a householder who, in spite of (and because of) his celebrity built houses, dwellings, homes, with an historic majesty about them.

When Monticello and Poplar Forest are compared to what came before – the great homes of the Virginia planters such as Stratford, Westover, Shirley, Mount Airy – Jefferson's work seems more respectful of the landscape. Monticello was built lower, with its dependencies literally burrowed into the site; Popular Forest is snug to its rise, a one-story pavilion on approach that, on its garden façade embraces its ornamental garden. If Jefferson was indeed the first great American architect, then he anticipates Frank Lloyd Wright (who proudly alluded to Jefferson, as he rarely did to other designers). Key to Wright's genius is his "organic architecture," and Jefferson's homes are Wrightian "organic" in the way they are grounded to their sites.

Appreciating a building is an analytical act. Yet the experience of looking at houses is also emotional – when the formality of the word "architecture" gives way to the softer concept of "home," the mind is swayed by the heart. And Jefferson's homes are personal places, expressions of his temperament and character. In the century after his death, Jefferson was raised on a pedestal, an unassailable and unrealistic marmoreal presence. In more recent years, the forbidding perfectability of that image has been repeatedly challenged while Monticello has become a national shrine – and as a place to see Thomas Jefferson, Architect, at his most experimental. Without attempting to elevate Jefferson onto another plinth, I would argue, at least in an architectural context, that he can be seen as a quintessential American type.

Jefferson had an overwhelming intellectual desire to impose a sense of order and reason on the world. One cannot help but discern in his building projects a willingness – nay, a compulsion – to change things, to tinker and test, to make better. It's significant that Jefferson instructed John Hemings to install the frieze ornaments at Poplar Forest years after he stopped visiting there. He was still imagining the place as all architects do, projecting a mental image of the building in his mind. He was dreaming of perfection, and to visit Monticello, Poplar Forest, and even the University is to glimpse the workings of his mind – and his heart – as he went about creating spaces for people.

While Jefferson's influence on American buildings has been demonstrably great, architectural historians have been less bullish in assessing Jefferson's contribution to world architecture. In truth, Thomas Jefferson, Architect, invented little. His genius was to adapt classical orders; good proportion; various design notions from French contemporaries; and native Virginia materials. He blended them all with a large dose of political aspiration.

His works are much more than assemblages of borrowed parts. There's a unity to his best buildings. Not that he himself was ever able to express clearly in words his architectural vision; as is often true, the descriptions of the designer are more opaque than the work itself. To wit: Jefferson described the Virginia State Capitol in his *Autobiography* as exemplifying his notion of "cubic architecture." Unfortunately, we can only guess at what he had mind because he never made explicit what he meant by "cubic." But we can contrast it with his "spherical" architecture, which he said was embodied by the Pantheon in Rome and his own Rotunda at the University of Virginia. And perhaps the Maison Carrée offers a clue, too. Its very name translates as the "square house." Jefferson was a man who thought in geometric terms, seeing beauty in the purity of plain figures like the cube and the sphere.

The surfaces he applied came, as he put it, from "a study of antient models." It must be noted that he knew ancient buildings through such Renaissance sources as Palladio, who came to them with their own prejudices and tastes (and even the Palladio Jefferson knew was adulterated, as Jefferson relied upon a British edition produced by Giacomo Leoni, an artist and architect who altered Palladio's plates and text to suit his own vision). In this book and others, the debt that Jefferson owed Palladio has been noted. He raised Palladio to the status of holy man – for Jefferson, it appears, the savant of Vicenza was the man who came back from his trips to Rome with the orders, the architectural commandments, writ in stone.

Yet as Jefferson grew more confident he couldn't help but let his independence flag fly. If the Academical Village is a remarkably coherent work – and certainly it is – that isn't because it's strictly Palladian, true to its classical sources, or even symmetrical. Though carefully balanced, Monticello is Jefferson's house, not Palladio's. These works are unmistakably Jefferson's own and they, together with Poplar Forest, best define his genius.

In assessing Jefferson's contribution to American architecture, I must succumb to the irresistible temptation to ask a couple of "What if?" questions. One is: *What if Jefferson hadn't become infatuated with the Roman Maison Carrée but had been smitten instead, say, with Chartres or Nôtre Dame?* Historic "what if?" questions are, on their face, absurd and perhaps you're thinking that, "No, of course not! Jefferson would never have fallen for a piece of ecclesiastical architecture." No doubt that's right (though the temples of ancient Rome and Greece weren't secular buildings). He certainly was schooled in things classical, having read and mastered Greek and Latin as a schoolboy; he was no medievalist.

But just suppose for a moment that Thomas Jefferson, Architect, the father of American Classicism, fell for a medieval cathedral . . . then mightn't he instead have been the father of American Gothic? It's a strange thought and obviously ahistorical. But think of the White House as resembling Westminster Abbey . . . and the Capitol as, say, Parliament by the Potomac. If his temperament and taste had tilted a different direction, American architecture would be different indeed, with public and private buildings alike distinctly asymmetrical and lined with pointed arches.

This discussion might really be the plot for a science fiction novel in disguise, but indulge me one more "What if?," a corollary to the first. Namely, *What if Jefferson had not been an architect . . . would the built environment in America look different today?* Imagine a streetscape with no columns and pediments. Beyond anyone else, Jefferson helped establish classical architecture as the proper mode not only for civic architecture in the young United States but as a stylish and desirable manner for domestic buildings, too. Its absence from the scene today is unthinkable.

If Jefferson's half century of work at Monticello can be characterized as an apprenticeship – and in my judgement the description is apt – then, inevitably, a related question arises: Can Jefferson, the perennial learner, a tyro and novice, also be described as a master?

It's a trick question. On the apprentice side there's Mr. Jefferson routinely seeking guidance from his architectural betters. He put Charles-Louis Clérisseau on the payroll to help design the Capitol in Richmond in the 1780s; during his presidency some twenty years later, he hired Benjamin Latrobe to be surveyor of the nation's public buildings. In the last decade of his life, Jefferson solicited Latrobe's and William Thornton's guidance as he developed his plan for his University. Throughout his life, Jefferson unhesitatingly consulted the writings of Palladio, Morris, Inigo Jones, Fréart de Chambray, and numerous other authorities whose books he kept near at hand.

In contrast, there are masterful buildings that are incontrovertibly the work of Jefferson: Monticello, Poplar Forest, Barboursville, and many structures at the University. And even the buildings that we know to have been collaborative efforts bear the unmistakable stamp of Jefferson.

I have come to think of the apprentice-master dichotomy as one of the chief charms of Thomas Jefferson, Architect. He wasn't superman; he had his share of tragic flaws and human frailties. In the realm of architecture, we are left with the paradox that he knew his limits yet aimed for the sky. He prided himself on being a lifelong student yet mentored dozens of designer-builders.

In truth, the roles of master and apprentice, particularly in an age of amateurism, were not mutually exclusive. To the close of even a very long life, one can act with confident authority at one moment and seek wise guidance the next. One can simultaneously be father *and* son (or mother and daughter). As William Wordsworth wrote in 1802, "The Child is father to the Man." The line is from Wordsworth's poem, "My Heart Leaps Up," which was an expression of Wordsworth's wish to retain a childish openness throughout life. Certainly Jefferson did. And it is for his youthful curiosity, his philosophical sense of inquiry, his historical consciousness, and his moral commitment to independence that we admire the man, the architect, Thomas Jefferson.

The approach to Poplar Forest with its waves of box hedge.

Notes and Acknowledgments

$\mathcal{M}$any distinguished ladies and gentlemen inhabit the Jeffersonian literature. Jefferson himself heads the list, followed by a band of biographers marching in close rank behind. In writing this book, I referred most often to Dumas Malone's magisterial six volume biography published under the rubric *Jefferson and His Time* (Boston: Little, Brown & Company, 1948 through 1981). Merrill Peterson's *Jefferson and the New Nation* (New York: Oxford University Press, 1970) is nearly as compendious. Joseph J. Ellis is a man whose own foibles may have made him particularly adept at explicating the paradoxes in Mr. Jefferson's character, and his book *American Sphinx* (New York: Alfred A. Knopf, 1997) makes a fine introduction to the mind of Jefferson, as well as being of manageable length for the casual reader.

While the subject of this book is, in some measure, the events of Jefferson's life, my debt is less to Messieurs Malone, Ellis and company than it is to the architectural historians, architects, conservators, and others concerned with understanding and restoring the buildings that, in ways direct and more tenuous, are linked to Jefferson.

The burly Fiske Kimball leads these troops, thanks largely to his masterpiece *Thomas Jefferson, Architect* (privately published in Boston in 1916, reprinted in New York by Da Capo Press in 1968). While Kimball put Jefferson on the architectural map, he can also be said to have done almost as much for the serious study of American architectural history. Colonial Revival predecessors had certainly admired early American buildings – thanks to McKim, Mead, and White, among others, the Colonial Revival was well underway by the time Kimball, a generation younger than Charles Follen McKim and Stanford White, came along, but he approached the study of early buildings with academic rigor. His scholarship contributed to early restoration efforts at Colonial Williamsburg, Stratford and Gunston Halls in Virginia, numerous major houses in Philadelphia and New England, as well as Monticello. Fiske Kimball's wife, Marie Goebel Kimball, became an accomplished scholar in her own right, publishing numerous books including a three-volume biography of Jefferson, and assisted Kimball in his various researches.

Thomas Jefferson's Architectural Drawings, compiled and with commentary and check list by Frederick Doveton Nichols (Charlottesville: Thomas Jefferson Memorial Foundation, Inc., 1961, 1995), is another essential reference to any student of Jefferson's architecture.

Though of minor scholarly value, three books devoted to Jefferson's architecture must be cited here as important early attempts to characterize his designs. The first is *Thomas Jefferson as an Architect and a Designer of Landscapes* by Dr. William Alexander Lambeth and Warren H. Manning (Boston: Houghton Mifflin Company, 1913). Lambeth, head of Buildings and Grounds at the University of Virginia, was prompted to write his book by his discovery of John Neilson's drawings in the Rotunda Library. *Thomas Jefferson: Architect and Builder* by I.T. Frary (Richmond: Garrett and Massie, 1931) and *Mr. Jefferson, Architect* by Desmond Guiness and Julius Trousdale Sadler, Jr. (New York: The Viking Press, 1973) are both books that cast a rather too inclusive net over central Virginia's "Jeffersonian" houses.

I am indebted to the next generation of scholars who have by no means completed their work on Jefferson. A number of them have generously answered my questions and thought aloud with me as I sought to express in a few pages what will surely be expanded upon by them in articles and later publications. Among their number is Travis McDonald, director of architectural restoration at Poplar Forest; John I Mesick of the firm of Mesick, Cohen, Wilson, Baker; Mark R. Wenger, Carl R. Lounsbury, Willie Graham, and Edward Chappell of Colonial Williamsburg; Professors Richard Guy Wilson, K. Edward Lay, Camille Wells, and Louis Nelson at the University of Virginia; Professor Duncan Stroik at the University of Notre Dame; Bryan Clark Green, architectural historian, Virginia Department of Historic Resources; James Murray Howard, former curator and architect for the Academical Village; and James E. Wootton, executive director of the Capitol Square Preservation Council.

For Jefferson's own writings I found *Thomas Jefferson: Writings* (New York: Library of America, 1984) a manageable and useful companion, as it contains his *Autobiography, Notes on the State of Virginia*, and a useful selection of his correspondence. I also perused his *Farm Books, Garden Books*, and miscellaneous other papers.

My appreciation must go to a range of other individuals – librarians, homeowners, public officials, and interested others – who answered my questions and recommended avenues of research. Among them are Quarto Hubbard at the Virginia Department of Historic Resources; Margaret O'Bryant at the Albemarle County Historical Society; Daniel Jordon, Susan Stein, Peter Hatch, Robert Self, William Beiswanger, Carrie Taylor, Kelly Fearnow, and Nancy Dudley at the Thomas Jefferson Foundation, Inc., caretakers for Monticello; Jack Robertson and Bryan Craig at The Jefferson Library at Monticello; and Nicholas Graham at the Massachusetts Historical Society. And with a special thanks to Wayne Mogielnicki who spent hours with Roger and me, at sun down and sun up, getting the images in this book.

At the University of Virginia, thanks to Louise Dudley, Director of University Relations; Carolyn Laquatra, administrator at the Rotunda; and especially the superb staff at the Fiske Kimball Fine Arts Library. Shooting images at the Capitol were made possible by the friendly cooperation of Joseph M. West, Jr., assistant director, Division of Engineering and Buildings, Department of General Services (exteriors), The Honorable Bruce Jamerson Clerk of the House of Delegates and The Honorable Susan Schaar Clerk of the Senate (interiors). Thanks are due to many people at the various sites including: George Costen and Carol Eltzroth, proprietors of Ampthill Plantation Bed and Breakfast; Luca Paschina at Barboursville; Elizabeth McClung, executive director, as well as Jacob Blosser and Eric Hutchinson, at Belle Grove; Jaime and Stanley Binsted, owners of Carrsbrook; Donna M. Wagner, Sales and Marketing Director at what is now Clifton: The Country Inn and Estate. At Edgehill, thanks to owners Ray and Barbara Graham and especially Gregory Graham; at Edgemont, owners Patrick and Arlette Monteiro de Barros, as well as Linda Dunn; to Ludwig Kuttner and Beatrix Ost at Estouteville; Carol Minetree and Philip Kiester at the Farmington Country Club; Carolyn Brooks, Executive Director of

Farmington, Kentucky; Joseph Smith Cochran III at Folly; Mrs. John C. Barrow at Frascati; Margaret Jones Perritt, curator at Rosewell; Charles and Randy Hill Carter as well as Taft Kiser, archaeologist, at Shirley Plantation; Addison B. Thompson at Tuckahoe; and, finally, our thanks and affection to the delightful Jane Moore at Shack Mountain.

Institutionally, I am indebted to the recordings of the Historic American Buildings Survey at the Library of Congress and to the Virginia Historic Landmarks Commission whose voluminous files on virtually all of the structures in this volume were key to my researches, both in locating some of the homes and of learning of their histories.

In addition to the sources cited above, I found much help at various stops along my Jeffersonian peregrinations. Chapter-by-chapter, the key ones include the following:

INTRODUCTION

The discussion of Palladio is indebted to many sources, including the master's own *The Four Books On Architecture*; the edition of choice is the new translation from Robert Tavernor and Richard Scofield (Cambrige, Massachusetts: MIT Press, 1997). Speaking of Professor Tavernor, his *Palladio and Palladianism* (London: Thames and Hudson, 1991) is arguably the best brief introduction to Palladian studies. I also found much to consider in the essay by Frank H. Sommer "Thomas Jefferson's First Plan for a Virginia Building" from *Papers on American Art,* John C. Millay, ed. (Maple Shade, NJ: Edinburgh Press, 1976). And John Summerson's BBC lectures on classicism, compiled as the *Classical Language of Architecture* (Cambridge, Massachusetts: The M.I.T. Press, 1963), is an accessible primer to the "grammar" of the orders. I am indebted to Camille Wells, specifically her article, "Virginia By Design: The Making of Tuckahoe and the Remaking of Monticello" (*Arris: The Journal of the Southeast Chapter the Society of Architectural Historians*, vol. 12, 2001) for explicating the connections between Tuckahoe and Jefferson's later architectural thinking; and to Mark R. Wenger and his essay, "Thomas Jefferson, Tenant" (*Winterthur Portfolio*, vol. 26, No. 4, 1991), which established a place for the disparate array of Jefferson's renovations within his body of architectural works.

Chapter 1 A TALE OF TWO MONTICELLOS

This book cannot claim to contain a definitive account of Monticello; rather, the modest goal in these pages has been to recount the story in brief within the context of Jefferson's architectural life. For the reader interested to learn more, however, there is a wealth of solid and engaging resources that contain much about Jefferson's principle residence.

No book on Jefferson's domestic architecture can be written without reference to *Jefferson and Monticello: The Biography of a Builder* (New York: Henry Holt and Company, Inc., 1988), Jack McLaughlin's absorbing and detailed account of Jefferson's fifty-four year building program on his hilltop. *Jefferson's Monticello* by William Howard Adams (New York, Abbeville Press, 1983) covers much of the same ground, but his book features numerous color images. Susan Stein's scholarly catalogue of Monticello's contents, *The Worlds of Thomas Jefferson at Monticello*, is accessible and rich with Jefferson surprises (New York: Harry N. Abrams, Inc., 1993).

I drew upon too many volumes in researching this chapter to cite them all, but a few of them proved notably useful. Jefferson's travels are recounted in detail in *Thomas Jefferson: American Tourist* by Edward Dumbauld (Norman, Oklahoma: University of Oklahoma Press, 1946). A useful collection of family letters is to be found in *The Family Letters of Thomas Jefferson*, Edwin Morris Betts, and James Adam Bear, Jr., eds. (Columbia: University of Missouri Press, 1966). The single best introduction to Jefferson's life in architecture and the arts is *The Eye of Thomas Jefferson*, William Howard Adams, editor (Charlottesville: Thomas Jefferson Memorial Foundation, Inc., and Columbia: University of Missouri Press, 1976). A companion volume to the National Gallery of Art bicentennial exhibit of the same name, this compendious volume offers a wealth of context, explicating the links between Jefferson and scores of the key cultural players of his time. Like any atlas of a certain age, it has become outdated in a few of its particulars but still provides a superb overview. In the same vein, *Jefferson and the Arts: an Extended View*, William Howard Adams, ed. (Washington, D.C.: National Gallery of Art, 1976) contains a range of valuable essays concerning Jefferson's forays into the world of arts and architecture.

One means of understanding the bookish Jefferson is to consider his library; in doing that, I found indispensable William Bainter O'Neal's *Jefferson's Fine Arts Library* (Charlottesville: University Press of Virginia, 1976).

Chapter 2   A NEW CAPITOL FOR THE COMMONWEALTH

This chapter is indebted to a number of sources, but first on the list must be "Thomas Jefferson and the Virginia State Capitol" by Mark R. Wenger *(The Virginia Magazine of History and Biography*, Vol. 101, No. 1, January 1993), in particular for the explication of the link between the floor plans of two Virginia Capitols. Fiske Kimball's writings come next, beginning with his doctoral research, which was variously published, originally in 1915 in three installments in the *Journal of the American Institute of Architects* under the title "Thomas Jefferson and the First Monument of the Classical Revival in America" and, more recently in book form as *The Capitol of Virginia* (Richmond: General Assembly of Virginia, 1989).

James E. Wootton, executive director of the Capitol Square Preservation Council, has been an invaluable source, both in conversation and thanks to his article, "Jefferson's Capitol and Capitol Square" (*Virginia Cavalcade*, Winter 2002). For the history of the Capitol model and the story of recent conservation efforts, my principal source was F. Carey Howlett's engaging article, "Thomas Jefferson's Model for the Capitol of Virginia" (*Virginia Cavalcade*, Winter 2002).

Paul F. Norton's essay, "Thomas Jefferson and the Planning of the National Capitol" in *Jefferson and the Arts* offers a thorough recounting of Jefferson's supervision of building in Washington. It was James Ackerman, in his enduring primer *Palladio* (New York: Penguin Books, 1966), who characterized Jefferson as having too obviously lifted his president's house design from the Villa Rotonda. The compendious two-volume *The President's House* by William Seale (Washington, D.C.: White House Historical Association, 1986) recounts the history of the president's dwelling in every particular.

Chapter 3   DWELLINGS FOR FRIENDS AND FAMILY

A wide range of people and publications contributed to this chapter. For buildings in Albemarle County, I have often relied upon Professor K. Edward Lay, both in person and in print (*The Architecture of Jefferson Country*, Charlottesville: University Press of Virginia, 2000). Another valuable source was Calder Loth's *The Virginia Landmarks Register* (fourth edition, Charlottesville: University Press of Virginia, 1999). *The Making of Virginia Architecture* by Charles F. Brownell, Calder Loth, William M.S. Rasmussen, and Richard Guy Wilson (Richmond: Virginia Museum of Fine Arts, 1992) provides a rich survey of surviving architectural drawings. The reference collection at the Kimball Library at the University of Virginia held many surprises, varying from real estate brochures to first-rate scholarly sources.

In examining individual sites, I drew upon a mix of materials. At Carrsbrook, I found useful material in Elizabeth Dabney Coleman's "Peter Carr of Carr's-Brook (1770-1815)" (*Magazine of Albemarle County History*, vol. 4, 1943-1944).

For the entry on The Residence, I must thank Leesa Campbell at the Woodberry Forest School, who has been supervising a recent renovation of The Residence and who, along with husband, Dennis M. Campbell, resides there. Special thanks, as well, to Louis P. Nelson, Assistant Professor of Architectural History, School of Architecture, University of Virginia, and his colleague Gwendolyn K. White, for talking with me about their findings as they prepare an historic structure report on the building. *Woodberry Forest: The Extended View* by Elizabeth Copeland Norfleet (Woodberry Forest School, 1979) chronicles the history of the school.

Regarding Edgemont, one source was Marian Page's *Historic Houses Restored and Preserved* (New York: Whitney Library of Design, 1976). Others were two papers prepared by students at the School of Architecture at the University of Virginia, which brought more rigor to the consideration of Edgemont and its principle restorer (*Edgemont, Albemarle County: A Jefferson Masterpiece or A Grigg Work of Art?* by Christine Desiree Holt, 1998, and *The Life and Career of* Milton *LaTour Grigg, FAIA* by Joseph Michael Lasala, 1990).

At Belle Grove, a key source was *Belle Grove: An Historic Structure Report* (March, 1996) prepared by Browne, Eichman, Dalgliesh, Gilpin and Paxton. I also drew with some caution upon an unpublished manuscript, "The History of Edgehill," loaned by Gregory Graham at Edgehill. My thanks, as well, to Professor K. Edward Lay for bringing Clifton to my attention as a "Jeffersonian" candidate. Finally, it was Travis McDonald who made the remark to me about napkin doodling.

Chapter 4 AN ESCAPE TO POPLAR FOREST

Today Travis C. McDonald, Jr., is the gatekeeper at Poplar Forest – and what a welcoming and wise presence he is, ever at the ready to share what he knows and talk with passion of his favored place. Like the restoration effort at Poplar Forest, this chapter is indebted to him. Among other essays of his that I have drawn upon are *Notes on the State of Poplar Forest*, volumes 1 and 2 (Forest, Virginia: The Corporation for Jefferson's Poplar Forest, 1991, 1994); "Poplar Forest: A Masterpiece Rediscovered" (*Virginia Cavalcade*, Winter, 1993); "Constructing Optimism: Thomas Jefferson's Poplar Forest" in *People, Power, Places,* Sally McMurry and Annmarie Adams, eds. (Knoxville: The University of Tennessee Press, 2000); and "Thomas Jefferson's Poplar Forest: Privacy Restored" (*Virginia Cavalcade*, Winter 2002). An essential reference to the property's past is the book *Poplar Forest and Thomas Jefferson* by S. Allen Chambers, Jr. (Forest, Virginia: The Corporation for Jefferson's Poplar Forest, 1993). In the last is reprinted the charming and invaluable letter of recollection from Ellen Wayles Randolph Coolidge regarding her girlhood visits with her grandfather to Poplar Forest. In conversations I have also learned much about Poplar Forest from Vince Fastabend, chief restoration craftsman, and, once again, John Mesick of Mesick, Cohen, Wilson, Baker, consulting architects for the restoration process.

Chapter 5 THE ACADEMICAL VILLAGE

The basic reference is *Thomas Jefferson's Academical Village: The Creation of an Architectural Masterpiece*, Richard Guy Wilson, editor (Charlottesville: Bayly Art Museum of University Press of Virginia, 1993). This book began life as an exhibition catalog, but its essays have proven of enduring interest. References to the University project abound in virtually all the major books cited above, but for particulars about the buildings today I drew upon the current edition of *The Campus Guide: University of Virginia* by Richard Guy Wilson and Sara A. Butler (New York: Princeton Architectural Press, 1999). The series of Historic Structure reports on some of the Pavilions prepared by Mesick, Cohen, Waite were also essential references, as was the draft report by S. Allen Chambers, Jr., on Pavilion VII.

Chapter 6   THE JEFFERSONIAN LEGACY
An early and important exploratory work devoted to Neilson, Dinsmore, Oldham, Perry, Dabney Crawford, and Phillips – both during Jefferson's lifetime and after – is Richard Charles Cote's dissertation, *The Architectural Workmen of Thomas Jefferson* (Boston University, 1986). Professor K. Edward Lay, together with a generation of his students at the University of Virginia, has also traced the lineage of Jefferson's builders in Albemarle County. Lay's essay, "Charlottesville's Architectural Legacy" in *The Magazine of Albemarle County History* (vol. 46, 1988, pp. 28-95) is a useful prelude to his magnum opus, *The Architecture of Jefferson Country* (Charlottesville: University Press of Virginia, 2000). Both are full to overflowing with the builders and buildings of Jefferson's home county of Albemarle. As with Chapter 3, *The Virginia Landmarks Register* and *The Making of Virginia Architecture* also rewarded close examination in writing this chapter. I am indebted to many of the home-owners cited above for granting us permission to examine and photograph their homes. The best current summary of the thinking on Bremo's "parentage" is *"they are spouting plans" for Bremo: The Making of a Virginia House in the New Republic* by Jennifer Danner Mauss (Master's thesis, School of Architecture, University of Virginia, 2000). Anne E. Bruder's article, "Evangelical Episcopalian Architecture" in *The Magazine of Albemarle County* History, vol. 55, 1997, was the key source for the story of Christ Episcopal Church, Charlottesville. For the Charlotte vs. Buckingham Courthouse debate, the definitive source is Delos Hughes' article, "The Charlotte County Courthouse: Attribution and Misattribution in Jefferson Studies," which appeared in *ARRIS: The Journal of the Southeast Chapter, Society of Architectural Historians*, vol. 4, 1993.

AFTERWORD
The closing words – and this entire book, in fact – came to be thanks to the first generations of students working on the subject of Thomas Jefferson, Architect. The most notable of them, in more or less chronological order, are Sidney Fiske Kimball, Milton LaTour Grigg, Thomas T. Waterman, and Professor Frederick Doveton Nichols. To them, the rest of us are indebted.

Index

Page references in boldface indicate the page number of an illustration or its caption. Thomas Jefferson is abbreviated as "TJ."